DOING IT MY WAY

For Jimmy Sellars
who loved Nilda + is a
great friend.
        with warm regards
        Red Blount
        Aug 1996

DOING IT MY WAY

by Winton M. "Red" Blount
with Richard Blodgett

GREENWICH PUBLISHING GROUP, INC.
LYME, CONNECTICUT

Produced and published by Greenwich Publishing Group, Inc., Lyme, Connecticut

Design by Tom Goddard Design

Prepress by Silver Eagle Graphics, Inc.

Library of Congress Catalog Card Number: 96-76552

ISBN: 0-944641-19-9

First Printing: May 1996

Photo credits:

p. 14	*Old B&SE Train Depot,* © Donard Trunton
p. 29	photograph by Paul Robertson
p. 47	photograph by Laurens Pierce
p. 56-57	(bottom) photographs by Jim McLain
p. 57	(top) courtesy of PPG Industries, Inc.
p. 75	UPI/Bettmann
p. 84	photograph by Sweeney South Commercial Photography
p. 89	UPI/Bettmann
p. 92	© Cal Alley
p. 101	courtesy of the United Postal Service
p. 104	(left) Illinois State Historical Library (right) UPI/Bettmann
p. 106	© Charles Brooks
p. 110	reprinted with permission from *U. S. News & World Report*
p. 112	© Charles Brooks
p. 116	(bottom) © Jim Palmer, Jr.
p. 117	(second from top) White House photograph
p. 121	White House photograph, reproduced from the copy in the Richard Nixon Library
p. 122	© Camille Vickers
p. 123	© Leviton
p. 126	(top) photograph by Laurens Pierce
p. 127	© Bud Hunter
p. 132	Archives Division - Texas State Library
p. 133	photograph by B. Artin Haig Studios
p. 142	(top) photograph by Paul Robertson
p. 162	© Jerry La Rocca
p. 169	© Ken Magee
p. 174	*Summer Twilight,* Stuart Davis, Montgomery Museum of Fine Arts, The Blount Collection
p. 175	*Flower Market,* © James Asher, The Blount Corporate Collection
p. 176	*The Bathers,* © John Asaro, The Blount Corporate Collection
p. 177	*New York Office,* Edward Hopper, Montgomery Museum of Fine Arts, The Blount Collection
p. 178	(left) *Ascent,* © Gary Price, The Blount Corporate Collection
p. 178	(right) *The Steelworker,* N. C. Wyeth, The Blount Corporate Collection
p. 187	© Timothy Hursley
p. 192	photograph by Paul Robertson
p. 194	© Timothy Hursley
p. 198	© Timothy Hursley
p. 201	photograph by Paul Robertson
p. 204	photograph by Paul Robertson
p. 205	*Fiesta at Ronda,* © John Asaro
p. 210	© Keeno
p. 212	(right) © George Halig

All other photographs and historical artifacts courtesy of Blount International, Inc. or Winton M. Blount.

Photography of Blount artifacts by Timothy J. Connolly.

Table of Contents

This book is dedicated to Carolyn, whose constant loving insistence inspired it, and to all the others who assisted in its preparation. It is also dedicated to all the employees of Blount International, without whom there would be no story to tell.

Introduction

AUTOBIOGRAPHY has been described as the art of writing about oneself without blushing. There are a few blushes in this book, but mostly it is full of great fun.

For years, I resisted the idea of telling the story of my business and my life. But I finally realized that I am my company's historian and only I can tell it right. The stories of corporations are a vital part of American history. All too often, however, first-hand accounts are lost forever because company founders never bothered to commit them to paper. I am determined this won't happen to Blount International.

For me, the business is an extension of my life: I live my work every day, and it's hard to separate the company from the man. So this book relates the story of my upbringing and personal interests as well as the history of Blount International.

The message of this book is simple: hire the best people, tell them what is expected, get out of their way, reward them well with incentives and hold them accountable.

There is a second message as well: business isn't everything. Enjoy life and take time to contribute to the greater good of society.

While those messages may sound serious, and they are, I don't think you will mind if you find some humor in these pages.

Winton M. "Red" Blount
April 1996

CHAPTER ONE

Growing Up in Alabama

I WAS LUCKY RIGHT FROM THE START. I GREW UP in small-town Alabama in a loving family that believed in hard work, entrepreneurship and public service. I can't imagine a better childhood. It was filled with joy, activity and family warmth.

When I look back at the people who influenced my life, I sometimes think of my grandfather, William Madison Blount. I never knew him. He died before I was born. Yet, the stories of his accomplishments made a deep impression on me as a youth. Around the turn of the century, my grandfather built a short-line railroad, the Birmingham & South Eastern, from Union Springs to Tallassee, Alabama. Attending an international conference of railroad executives in Canada some 15 years later, he fell into conversation with the president of the Canadian Pacific, who asked, "Well, Mr. Blount, how long is your railroad?" My grandfather answered, "Fifty miles." The president of the Canadian Pacific then suggested, "The only difference between our railroads is that yours is 50 miles long and mine is 5,000." To which my grandfather replied, "Oh no, Sir Henry, there's one other difference. I *own* mine." As a youngster, I loved to hear that story. I wanted to follow in my grandfather's footsteps and start a business when I grew up.

During World War I, when railroads in the United States were nationalized, my grandfather went to Washington as a dollar-a-year man to run the nation's short-line railroad system. As the story goes, my grandmother, whom we all called "Bunny," stayed behind in

Below, I was a happy child growing up in small-town Alabama. Opposite, this picture was taken when I was in my teens and shows my auburn hair, from which I got my nickname, Red. Left, my grandfather, William Madison Blount, built the short-line Birmingham & South Eastern Railroad from Union Springs to Tallassee, Alabama.

Alabama, but she soon became suspicious that my grandfather, who was charming and dapper, might be up to no good. She set off secretly by train for the nation's capital and, once there, tailed my grandfather incognito for an entire week. Her sleuthing ended happily: she found nothing to justify her suspicions and returned to Alabama a contented woman. We Blounts are like that: relentless to a fault.

When my grandfather died in 1919, my father, Winton "Beau" Blount, took over as president of the family-owned B&SE, known popularly as the Bump & Slide Easy. My father had just returned from France after serving in World War I. He was a real pistol — short, stocky, energetic, successful in business, always ready to support a worthy cause. He and I were very close. He encouraged me to be self-reliant and make the most of my life. Many times he said to me, "Son, I don't care if you are a peanut vendor on the corner, just be the best peanut vendor you can be." That statement was burned into my brain and has guided me in all that I have done. I never translated his advice into wanting to be wealthy or run the biggest business. I simply wanted to be the best. Whatever success I have achieved in life is a direct result of never settling for second best.

My father and mother visited me at Turner Field in Albany, Georgia, when I was in the Army Air Corps during World War II. My father had a tremendous influence on my life, encouraging me to be the best at whatever I did. The newspaper article describes some of my grandfather's successful business ventures.

THE BULLOCK COUNTY BREEZE, Union Springs, Ala., December 16, 1902.

W. M. Blount.

W. M. Blount, the subject of this photograph, was born in Decatur County, Georgia, October 10th, 1854, his father was a native of England. Mr. Blount came to Union Springs in the Fall of 1896, entered the mercantile business with a large stock of goods, and by close attention to business, with a great amount of energy, soon placed himself as one of the city's foremost merchants.

Mr. Blount is in his sphere, however, as a promoter of important enterprises, and soon after his coming here he saw the great need of a competing railroad, and at once began his efforts to build the Union Springs & Northern Road. This enterprise had been discussed by our citizens for many years, and its great possibilities realized by all, but the scheme needed a leader, a man that knew where to apply for money and railroad influence for money. Mr. Blount began the effort, and with but little money expended by our citizens, the road was completed. The credit for this road, which has already done so much for our city, in advancing the value of property and increasing our population, is due absolutely to Mr. Blount. He is not a man to remain idle, but is

even now laying his plans for more enterprises and industries. While living in Bainbridge, Ga., Mr. Blount organized the Bainbridge State Bank, in 1882, was President of the same for ten years, and while President of this Bank, organized and built the following enterprises: Bainbridge Ice Factory, Bainbridge Compress Company and the Edison Electric Light Company.

Mr. Blount is congenial, makes friends readily, and has confidence, esteem and admiration of a public that realizes his great assistance to it. The people of Union Springs are justly proud of Mr. Blount, who has done so much to promote her interests, and are glad to claim him as a citizen and resident.

FAMILY HERITAGE OF POLITICS

One of my father's great passions was politics, a love I inherited from him. His greatest political achievement came in 1943 when he got his good friend, George Andrews, elected to the U.S. Congress. George was a lawyer in our hometown, Union Springs, and served as circuit solicitor for Bullock, Barbour and Dale counties. He was a small, feisty fellow with a gravelly voice. In 1943, when my father suggested he run for Congress, George was serving as a navy lieutenant at Pearl Harbor. George never set foot in Alabama during the entire contest; my father organized and managed the campaign completely. The contest soon evolved into a neck-and-neck race between George and a man named Johnson from Dothan in the southeast corner of the state. On election night, as the results came in, George camped out in the navy communications center at Pearl Harbor to listen by short-wave radio to newscasts from Alabama. First came a report in which my father was quoted as saying that George had won by 3,000 votes. Then came one in which my father said George had won by 2,000. A while later, my father said 1,300. George's navy friends allowed that if Mr. Blount didn't stop talking, and the election board didn't stop counting, George would never make it to the Congress. Finally, when all the ballots had been counted, George had won by 300 votes, embarking on a Congressional career of nearly three decades.

CHILDHOOD IN UNION SPRINGS

I was born in 1921 in Union Springs, Alabama, population 3,000. Located 40 miles east of Montgomery, Union Springs is the seat of Bullock County and a commercial center for local agriculture. In my youth, it was straight out of a Norman Rockwell illustration: there was one paved street, everybody knew everybody else and doors were left unlocked throughout the night. King cotton dominated the surrounding landscape. Each fall, piles upon piles of cotton bales were stacked by the railroad depot and up and down Main Street, awaiting shipment to places I could only imagine. At the end of Main Street was the Confederate monument, a favorite gathering place for older men playing checkers. During World War II, when I was a pilot in the Army Air Corps stationed at Turner Field in Georgia, I sometimes flew over Union Springs and "buzzed" the town. One week I was home on leave and was driving down Main Street. As I drove around the monument, a plane swooped down from the sky, barely above the treetops. Mr. Rainer, one of the checker players, shouted, "There's that damn Red Blount again." I yelled out my car window, "Not me

I never thought the world would get to see me naked.

My grandmother, "Bunny" Blount, was a talented pianist. She lived near us in Union Springs and was always fun to be around.

this time, Mr. Rainer. I'm right here in my car."

Fires were big events in Union Springs, as they are in many small towns. Whenever the town fire bell rang, crowds would chase after the fire engine to watch the action. With most buildings being constructed of wood, with coal-burning railroad engines spitting forth sparks and with volunteer fire departments trying their best using rudimentary equipment, the railroad depot caught fire on three separate occasions in the 1920s, each time burning to the ground. Such were the perils of small-town life in that era.

Because my father ran the railroad, which he owned with his brother and two sisters, we were one of the prominent families in town. We weren't rich, but we were financially comfortable, even at the depths of the Great Depression. We were a close-knit group: my father, mother, younger brother Houston and younger sister Barbara, in addition to myself. Other relatives — including my paternal grandmother, Bunny (who died in 1936), and my father's sister, "Aunt Bill" (short for Wilda) — also lived in Union Springs. Members of the extended Blount clan were constantly visiting one another.

We were a church-going family, as was true of virtually everyone in the community. My grandfather Blount was a Baptist, my grandmother Blount an Episcopalian. The way they worked it out was to raise the boys as Baptists and the girls as Episcopalians. As a result, my father was a Baptist and I grew up in the Baptist Church.

Because my brother Houston and I are only 11 months apart in age, we were almost like twins and were great pals, although we also scrapped like a couple of frisky puppies. As all of Houston's many friends know, he is a wonderful raconteur and the life of any party. Even in his youth, he was known for his engaging wit and ability to tell a good story, true or embellished. He was also quite a prankster. When the schoolhouse caught fire in the middle of the night, just about the whole town turned out to watch the blaze. Seeing the school in flames, Houston raced home, returned with his books and tossed them into the fire. As I recall, our parents were not too amused.

My mother, Clara Belle Chalker Blount, was an extraordinary woman — tall, beautiful, intelligent. She was from Ozark, Alabama, where her father worked as a clerk in the law department of a railroad. Like my father, she was a loving parent and strict disciplinarian.

During the 1920s and 1930s, we lived in a small, comfortable, one-story house on what was called "the hill." Across the street was a plum orchard. And the nearness of that orchard was the bane of the Blount boys' existence. Like a lot of youngsters in Union Springs, Houston and I sometimes did things our parents thought we

My brother Houston and I were probably three or four years old when this photograph was taken. I'm on the left. We were — and are — great pals, although as kids we sometimes battled like a couple of frisky puppies. That's me in the oval picture.

shouldn't. Whenever we got caught, punishment was meted out swiftly: Father or Mother would dispatch the wayward son to the orchard to bring back a lengthy plum switch covered with nodes. The switch would then be applied briskly across that very same son's bottom. I was switched more often than I care to remember. Switching was common in the South. Children accepted it, albeit none too happily, and nobody ever suggested it was some form of child abuse.

One reason I sometimes got switched was for playing hooky from school. And one of the reasons I played hooky was to sneak into the county courthouse whenever it was in session every two or three months. I loved the drama of the courtroom and even dreamed for a time of becoming a lawyer. I witnessed many fascinating cases, but none more sensational than the trial of the son of a prominent local family who was charged with rape. I still remember George Andrews, the man my father later helped get elected to Congress, pointing his finger straight at the defendant and proclaiming with fire and brimstone dripping from every word, "He ought to go to the electric chair!" Well, he didn't go to the electric chair, but he was convicted and did go to jail.

THE FAMILY RAILROAD BUSINESS

As I mentioned earlier, my father was an astute businessman. When he took charge of the B&SE railroad in 1919, following my grandfather's death, it was in hock to the bond houses in New York. A turning point came in the early 1920s, when the Alabama Power Company decided to build a dam near Alexander City. Seizing the opportunity, my father extended the railroad 10 miles to the construction site, and it was over those tracks that all the sand, gravel, steel and other materials were transported, generating a surge of revenue for the B&SE lasting several years. My father used this money to repay the railroad's bonds.

By the early 1930s, however, the B&SE was suffering from the effects of the Great Depression. My father had built a sand and gravel plant and a concrete pipe plant along the line to generate revenue for the railroad, and these were doing reasonably well. But the rail-

The northern terminus of the family-owned B&SE railroad was at this depot in Tallassee, Alabama. The depot was built in the early 1900s and was a major point for freight and passenger service for more than half a century. Beginning in the 1920s, passengers boarded liveried coaches at the depot for excursions to Lake Martin and Montgomery. Businesses shipped minnows, shotguns, live chickens, cotton goods and other products from this station. Similar depots were built on the B&SE at Eclectic, Asbury, Liverpool, Milstead and Union Springs.

road itself was having a tough go of it. The seven northernmost miles of track remained profitable: a big cotton mill in Tallassee, Alabama, at the railroad's northern end, shipped all its goods over those seven miles to the railroad junction at Milstead for transfer to the main line of the Atlanta & West Point. However, the rest of the B&SE was by now under-used. My father was struggling with the railroad, making money on the seven-mile segment but spending it just about as fast to maintain the other 43. In the mid-1930s, my father went to see his friend, Mr. Wickersham, president of the Atlanta & West Point. He came home that night and made a shocking statement. Mr. Wickersham had told him, "Beau, if you have cancer in your right arm, are you going to sit there and let it eat up your body, or are you going to cut off your right arm?" Accepting Mr. Wickersham's advice, my father decided to take up the money-losing 43 miles of track and close that section of the line forever. I was then 13 years old. It was early summer, school vacation had started, and I asked my father if I could join the work crew taking up the rails. He was more than happy to oblige. I earned 10 cents an hour, which I thought was pretty good, working initially as a water boy for the crew and soon joining in the hard labor — picking up spikes and steel plates, then helping with the rails, the most backbreaking job of my life. After the B&SE was pruned to seven miles, it earned a nice profit and continued to do so until the late 1940s, when rail transportation began to be overtaken by cars and trucks.

In 1936, my father bought another short-line railroad, the Tuskegee, which ran about eight miles from Tuskegee Institute in the city of Tuskegee to the main line of Mr. Wickersham's railroad, the

Bottom, employees of the B&SE posed in the 1950s with the railroad's first and only diesel engine. My uncle, Colonel Roberts Blount, the railroad's president, is standing on the engine. That's me, fourth from the left in front of the engine. Below, Bill Pullen, president of United States Fidelity & Guaranty Company, joined me in a B&SE engine. USF&G was Blount's bonding company for many years, supporting our growth in construction.

Atlanta & West Point. He then built a sand and gravel plant and an asphalt plant on the Tuskegee line to generate traffic. Mr. Runette, a delightful older man, managed the Tuskegee Railroad for my father and owned a small percentage of both the railroad and the sand and gravel plant. Each of these operations — the Tuskegee Railroad, the sand and gravel plant and the asphalt plant — was profitable in its own right and supported the others. As I said, my father was an astute businessman.

As our family prospered, my father and his two sisters — Aunt Bill in Union Springs and Aunt Kathleen in Columbia, South Carolina — bought land in Myrtle Beach, South Carolina, which was then largely undeveloped, and built a house, the interior of which was paneled in beautiful "pecky" cypress wood. Each summer, we would vacation for a week or two at Myrtle Beach. Because of our house there, and as a result of friendships made through Aunt Kathleen, my parents knew many people in South Carolina. One of my father's closest friends was Alvin Lumpkin, a distinguished lawyer who briefly represented South Carolina in the United States Senate after being appointed by the governor to fill a vacancy. My father loved to sing, as did Mr. Lumpkin, and they sometimes rang each other up just to sing together long-distance over the phone between Union Springs and South Carolina — or even California, when Mr. Lumpkin traveled to that state. This was in the days when receiving a phone call from across the country was quite exotic, especially to a wide-eyed youngster. Houston, Barbara and I are still close to our Carolina cousins, whose father was a fun-loving Englishman.

AN EARLY TASTE FOR WORK

Because my father was active in politics all his adult life and was well liked and respected, the short-line railroad owners of Alabama asked him to represent their interests in the state legislature. He served as a kind of unpaid lobbyist. It was through this connection that I became a page in the legislature when I was 10 years old. This led to some unusual experiences.

In the early 1930s in Alabama, you didn't need a license to drive. Children drove when they were as young as nine or ten, and nobody so much as blinked an eye when a youngster cruised by at the wheel of a car or a truck. I was soon enlisted to chauffeur two elderly members of the state legislature: Mr. Charlie Norman, the speaker of the house, and Colonel T. Sydney Frazier, a member of the state senate, both of whom lived in Union Springs. Three times a week, I drove them 40 miles to the state capitol in Montgomery, making the return trip each night at about 10 p.m. after the legislature had completed its activities for the day. It may seem incongruous: a 10-year-old chauffeur driving two of the most powerful men in Alabama, bouncing along on the gravel roads (the road between Union Springs and Montgomery was not yet paved), trying to avoid an occasional stray cow (Alabama did not yet have fence laws to keep livestock off the highways). However, I took my responsibilities very seriously and even managed to get my VIP commuters back and forth without a single accident! Working as a page, I earned $4 a day seven days a week, even though the legislature was in session only three days a week. I thought I was in heaven.

Nonetheless, there were disappointments. One time, a member of the state legislature, knowing I had plenty of money from my per diem, asked if he could borrow $50 (equivalent to several hundred dollars today). I got permission from my father to make the loan, and the deal was promptly closed. Subsequently, the man left the legislature and was elected to the U.S. Congress, and he never did pay me back that $50. Nearly 40 years later, when I went to Washington as postmaster general in the Nixon administration, the fellow was still in Washington, though no longer a member of Congress. I happened to tell some Washington colleagues about the $50, without disclosing the rascal's identity, and they blurted out his name even before the last words had left my mouth. It turned out he was infamous, even by Washington standards, for the ill-use of other people's money.

As a page in the Alabama legislature, I was assigned to five members of the legislature. One of my tasks was to pick up their paychecks at the comptroller's office every two weeks and deliver them personally to the five lawmakers. It was the middle of the Depression, and, like everybody else, they were squeezed for money and wanted

Portraits of Houston, right, and me from our teenage years in the 1930s suggest a couple of serious young men determined to succeed in life. Although we were less than a year apart in age, our personalities could not have been more different. Houston was a gregarious raconteur, while I was shy.

Above, I graduated from Union Springs High School in 1938. That's me, back row, far right, in our senior class picture. Right, in my sophomore year our basketball team had a winning record and went to the playoffs. I'm in the front row next to the coach. To my left is Sam Wilson, who became one of our company's first employees in 1947 and spent nearly 40 years at Blount, retiring in 1984 as vice president in charge of business development.

their paychecks as quickly as possible. One time, when I got to Mr. Pitts, then the sole Republican in the Alabama legislature, I didn't have his paycheck and had no idea what had become of it. I was speechless. He started raising Cain, and I became very frightened. My father used to stay at the Exchange Hotel on Dexter Avenue, so I hopped on a streetcar and went to the hotel, where I found him in the barbershop getting a shave. I sat down to wait, and he kind of watched me and saw I was about to cry. When he was done, he said, "Let's get out of here," and took me to his room. I told him what had happened and sobbed that I didn't have any idea where the check had gone. My father said, "Well, Son, let's just go up there and see what the story is." So we went back to the comptroller's office and found that Mr. Pitts had given instructions to the comptroller to send his pay directly to a bank in his hometown of Clanton, Alabama — and had forgotten all about it! Mr. Pitts was quite embarrassed when he realized what had happened, and I learned a valuable lesson: other people's money is very important. I should have known what I had in my hand before I left the comptroller's office.

PASSION FOR SPORTS

Even though our family was well off, hard work remained the order of the day for the Blount boys. Not only was I expected to do household chores and keep up with schoolwork, but I also had a series of jobs as a youngster beginning at age 10 — in the legislature, in a local store, on the railroad, at my father's sand and gravel plants, at his asphalt plant. I always dug right in and gave my very best. In fact, by the time I was 16, my father called me his "40-year-old son" — not only because I looked older than I was, but also because I worked so hard.

However, there was one activity I loved even more than work, and that was sports. I had the build of an athlete: tall, lean and limber. Houston and I were always playing football, basketball, baseball... whatever the sport of the moment happened to be. Although schools and social life in Alabama were strictly segregated, informal pick-up games in Union Springs were not. Through sports, I got to know teenagers of all backgrounds and became friends with many. One of my friends was J. C. Blackman, the son of our longtime family cook, Leola Blackman. He and I were the same age and often played baseball together. We remained close until he died in the 1960s, sadly not yet 50 years old.

I earned letters in football, basketball and baseball each of my four years at Union Springs High School. Senior year, I played running back on the football team while Houston, a junior, played quarterback. We went undefeated, untied and unscored upon, and I earned all-state honorable mention.

Several star athletes before me at Union Springs had gone to Staunton Military Academy in Virginia for one year before enrolling in college. I chose that same path. I continued to play football at Staunton and enjoyed the academics, as well. The teachers were superb, and I am convinced I learned more in that one year than in all my other years of formal education combined.

Leaving Staunton, I entered the University of Alabama in the fall of 1939. I tried out for the Bama football team, one of the most powerful in the country. It quickly became apparent that my six-foot-two-inch, 145-pound string-bean frame was not built for colli-

We had a terrific football team my senior year in high school, completing the season undefeated, untied and unscored upon. I was a lean, speedy running back, and Hunky Shell, right, was an offensive guard. Oh, how I loved those big offensive linemen who did all the dirty work.

sions with 250-pound defensive tackles. Moreover, I didn't have a taste for college academics. After a year and a half, I called my father and told him I was wasting my time and his money being in college. He didn't try to talk me out of quitting. He just said that if I dropped out of college I had to work — which was exactly what I wanted to do.

His relaxed attitude about my leaving college was almost certainly influenced by his relationship with his own father. Both of them were strong-willed, and their relationship was tempestuous. My father went to Howard College (now called Samford University) in Birmingham, Alabama, playing on the Howard football team, but dropped out after three years when he and his father had a severe disagreement. I don't know what the disagreement was about, but I do know that my father struck out for California and worked there building railroads, supervising a crew of Chinese laborers in the Sierra Nevada mountains. He stayed in California two or three years before returning home and reconciling with his family. I am strong-willed, too, and I think my father was always very concerned that we be able to work out our differences and never risk becoming alienated.

In any event, I never did get a bachelor's degree, although back then, of course, being a college graduate wasn't nearly as important as it is today.

So in January 1941, at age 19, I left the University of Alabama, having completed one-and-a-half years as an engineering major, to manage an asphalt plant in Selma, Alabama, in which my father had part ownership. At the time, the plant was supplying asphalt for the paving of Craig Field, an Army Air Corps base in Selma. The contractor at the air base was Hoke Vandergriff, a rough, tough character who had played catcher and left field on the Union Springs semi-pro baseball team in the 1930s. Mr. Vandergriff worked very hard and was very demanding of his people. One of my vivid recollections is of a broken-down tractor parked in the middle of a scorching field in the summer. Mr. Vandergriff did not let his employees repair tractors

After graduating from high school, I spent a year at Staunton Military Academy in Virginia before enrolling at the University of Alabama. That's me, far left in this picture, with a couple of buddies in the atrium of the barracks at Staunton. As a young man, I played all kinds of sports, including golf.

in the shade. When a tractor stopped running, he insisted they repair it in the full blast of the sun so they would have plenty of incentive to fix it quickly and get back to their regular work. Another of my recollections of Mr. Vandergriff dates back to the mid-1930s, when he bought asphalt from my father's Tuskegee plant. After paying his truck drivers each Saturday, Mr. Vandergriff would invariably start a craps game and win much of the money right back. I was 15 years old and wondered why in the world the drivers would allow themselves to be drawn into a craps game every week. But jobs were hard to get in the middle of the Depression.

At the Selma plant in 1941, we began producing asphalt each day at 4 a.m. and began loading Mr. Vandergriff's trucks by 5 a.m. Liquid asphalt, sand and gravel were the main raw materials. One day, the liquid asphalt didn't arrive by railroad from Louisiana. I was frantically phoning the supplier, trying to find out where it was, when all of a sudden I saw a car speeding down the dirt road toward the plant. It was Mr. Vandergriff in his Lincoln Zephyr, and he jumped out of that car and made a beeline for me, absolutely furious, wanting to know where his asphalt was. I tried to explain the problem, but he didn't want to listen to any of that. He just chewed me out like nothing you ever heard. Believe me, I never ran out of asphalt again. When I went into the contracting business after the war, Mr. Vandergriff always claimed he was responsible for my success because of the tongue-lashing he gave me that morning.

WARTIME SERVICE

On Sunday, December 7, 1941, I was at the Paramount Theater in downtown Montgomery, watching *Sergeant York*, starring Gary Cooper as the World War I Medal of Honor hero. The movie was suddenly interrupted, the lights were turned on and news of the Japanese attack on Pearl Harbor was announced. It was an unbelievable shock! The next day I went to Maxwell Field in Montgomery and enlisted as a pilot cadet in the Army Airs Corps, spending the next four years in the service, flying B-29s and B-25s. (The latter was the type of plane used by General Jimmy Doolittle's strike force, which took off from an aircraft carrier in the Pacific just four months after Pearl Harbor and bombed Tokyo, dealing a huge psychological blow to the Japanese. Until that moment, the Japanese had never imagined Americans could bring the war to their homeland. Doolittle's raid so unnerved the Japanese that they recalled several fighter groups from other theaters to defend the capital.) A year and a half after I joined the army, Houston enlisted as a pilot cadet in the navy. I

I was a flight instructor in the Army Air Corps during the early years of World War II, embarking on a lifelong love affair with aviation. I'm second from the left. We called this type of trainer plane the "bucket of bolts," because it tended to shake, rattle and roll.

had a particular reason for wanting to be a pilot. While living in Selma, managing the asphalt plant, I boarded at the house of Mrs. Rainer, who had family in Union Springs. Three first lieutenants from Craig Field also boarded at her house. They were the kings of the walk: they had convertible cars and wore fancy uniforms, and the girls adored them. I wanted to be a pilot, no question about it.

I took to aviation quickly and easily, embarking on a lifelong love affair with flying. Nine months after enlisting, shortly after having earned my wings in November 1942 at Turner Field in Albany, Georgia, I was transferred to Maxwell Field in Montgomery to attend central instructors school, where I learned to train other pilots. Those attending the school were required to fly a low-altitude course over Alabama and Georgia. Low altitude? Taking them at their word, I flew under a bridge on the Chattahoochee River and was caught by one of the instructors. I spent Christmas 1942 confined to base. (I loved to fly and was always pushing the envelope, and maybe that is one reason I have succeeded in business. I have never been fazed about trying new things.)

That same year, when I was in the final phase of flight training, I married my high school sweetheart, Mary Katherine Archibald. Those who know me now may find this difficult to believe, but I was a very shy child, totally the opposite of my gregarious brother, Houston. In grade school, Mary Katherine could make me blush just by staring at me. My nickname, Red, comes from the color of my hair (when I had some), but could just as easily have come from the color of my face at moments like those. Mary Katherine and I were married for more than 30 years and raised five children — Winton, Tom, Sam, Kay and Joe — to whom we both remain close. However, there was tension in the marriage from the beginning, and we eventually went through a bitter divorce. I will come back to that later in this book.

I married my first wife, Mary Katherine, during the war, and we had five children. I was a mighty proud papa when our youngest son, Joe, was born in 1955. My other children, from left, are Winton, Sam, Tom and Kay.

In 1945, I was about to get my chance to fly in combat as the pilot of a B-29 Superfortress. I'm at the left in this picture with my crew. We trained for four months, flying mock missions up the East Coast to "bomb" Boston.

However, the Japanese surrendered just as we were to be sent to the Pacific, and we never did see combat duty.

On completing central instructors school at Maxwell Field, I was assigned to Turner Field in Georgia to train other pilots. The trainer planes we used at Turner Field did not have any of the modern technology found in today's aircraft. The instruments were not much more than "needle, ball and air speed." A colonel who was a former Eastern Air Lines senior pilot was the first person to fly into a hurricane. He was in charge of flight training at a base in Columbus, Mississippi, and flew into the hurricane in an AT-6 advanced single-engine trainer. I was very impressed. Not much was known about flying conditions in thunderstorms, either. I started flying into them, learning about wind, altitude, clouds, etc. Sometimes the plane, caught in a draft, would soar or plunge 5,000 to 8,000 feet in a few

Capt. G.L. Dressler

In 1943 and 1944, while stationed at Turner Field in Georgia, I was assigned to this advisory board which trained flight instructors. I'm at the far left. We were quite a high-spirited group. Herb Farnsworth, next to me, set an Army Air Corps record by flying 255 hours in one month. He later became the senior pilot of Delta Air Lines and died in his fifties of a heart attack. Later in the war, Captain Dressler, second from the right, came back to Turner Field from temporary duty in Dayton, Ohio, talking mysteriously about plans to attack Japan with a single airplane carrying a single bomb. The idea seemed astonishing. That was the first inkling I had of the atomic bomb.

seconds. I loved flying in bad weather. Even though planes did not have any of the modern landing instruments we have today, I flew when visibility was as low as 50 feet.

A few months after being assigned to Turner Field to train pilots, I was promoted to an advisory board to train the trainers, serving in that role until January 1945, when I was again assigned to Maxwell Field, this time to learn to fly a B-29 Superfortress in preparation for combat duty. From the start of the war, I had wanted to fly in combat, and my chance had finally arrived — or so I thought. With the completion of B-29 training, I was sent to Lincoln, Nebraska, where 10,000 airmen had assembled to form crews and depart for combat in the Pacific. The air base at Lincoln had three officers clubs, all of tarpaper construction. I walked into one my first Sunday there. Card games were going hot and heavy at every table in sight, and soon I joined a game of straight poker. During the course of that afternoon, I had one hand with three kings and another with a full house. Both times I bet big and lost. I ended up blowing $500, every penny I had, and forever lost my appetite for gambling. I gamble in business all the time. I know the risks and feel confident I can win. I never gamble at cards. I see no reason to trust my fate to Lady Luck.

At Lincoln, I picked up my crew of 10. We went to Savannah, Georgia, for crew training prior to leaving for the Pacific to join the war against Japan. However, while in Savannah, the war came to an end, and I never did get sent overseas or fly in combat.

AFTER THE WAR

Two days after D-Day 1944, when I was still stationed in Albany, Georgia, my father suffered a massive heart attack. I rushed home, but he was in a coma and died shortly thereafter. He was 53. He and I had always been extremely close. His death was a terrible blow to the entire family, particularly to my sister, Barbara. My father adored her.

On returning from military service in November 1945, my first concern was to restore my father's sand and gravel business, which now belonged to my mother and had fallen on hard times following his death. Houston and I wanted to bring the business back to profitability so Mother could be financially secure.

At the same time, we thought about going into business for ourselves. One idea, which first came to me when I was 15 years old, was the contracting business. My father, in selling the output of his gravel, asphalt and concrete pipe plants, often attended public works contract lettings in Montgomery. Time and again, he would return home frustrated by what he saw to be misrepresentations and double-dealings by contractors and other suppliers. Although my father was a keen businessman who drove a hard bargain, he believed in honest dealings and was always dismayed by those who didn't. I kept saying to him, "Dad, instead of selling sand and gravel to the general contractors, why don't you become a contractor yourself?" He didn't take my advice at the time, although he did build two projects in partnership with others during World War II: a German prisoner-of-war camp in Aliceville, Alabama, and a 29-mile railway system at a holding and reconsignment depot in Montgomery.

As I looked ahead in late 1945, I thought about my father's advice to be the best peanut vendor there is. I did not have any grand plan for building a huge company. I just wanted to be the best. That was very much my ambition as I returned to civilian life following the war.

Our father was very proud of Houston and me. He visited with us during the war at Turner Field in Albany, Georgia. Houston, a Navy pilot, was stationed at Pensacola, Florida, at the time of this picture. I had flown to Pensacola in a B-25 to bring him to Georgia. Our father died of a heart attack a few months after this photograph was taken. He was just 53 years old when he passed away.

CHAPTER TWO

Blount Brothers Construction Company Takes Root

BLOUNT INTERNATIONAL, INC., WAS BORN IN AN unusual way. On returning from the Second World War, Houston and I began managing the businesses our mother had inherited from our father. Seeking to rebuild these businesses, I went to Atlanta to the War Surplus Administration office, which was selling all kinds of surplus equipment. Initially, I bought a crane and two Euclid haulers for use in the sand and gravel operation. A few weeks later, I was back in Atlanta shopping for other equipment when a War Surplus Administration employee asked me out of the blue, "How would you like to buy four Caterpillar D-7 tractors that have never been used?" Taking a look, I found them to be brand-new machines with scrapers — perfect for moving dirt and grading roads. And they were available for only $7,000 apiece, perhaps half the market price. Even though we had no use for them in Mother's sand and gravel operation, I immediately bought all four tractors. When I got back to Union Springs and told Houston about my purchase, he said, "What in the hell are we going to do with that stuff?" Having thought the matter through on my return trip from Atlanta, I replied, "We're going into the contracting business." And that is how Blount Brothers Construction Company (the original name of Blount International) came into being.

Although we didn't have much money, I wasn't worried about getting $28,000 to pay the War Surplus Administration. Thanks to my father's fine reputation, the Blounts were known in Union

Opposite, this picture of Houston and me was taken at our company office in the Frank Leu Building in Montgomery after we moved there in the 1950s. Houston was still a partner in the business, even though he had taken a leave of absence to work with our uncle. Houston never did return to Blount and went on to a highly successful career at Vulcan Materials, eventually becoming its CEO. Below, the model of a Caterpillar D-7 tractor (the type of machine with which we started Blount) was given to me by John Panettiere, Blount's CEO since 1993.

Springs as people you could count on, and I rightly figured we could borrow the entire amount from the local bank, which was owned by Mr. Frank Mosely, a close friend of my father and mother. We did just that, with Mother guaranteeing the loan. She always had enormous confidence in us, and she signed the endorsement without the slightest hesitation, even though she was putting a large portion of her assets at risk. (We had that loan for several years without repaying any of the principal. One day, however, Mr. Mosely asked me to come down to the bank and he said, "I think it's time you started paying back." So we did, with a twist. Mr. Morgan, who had previously worked for Mr. Mosely at the bank in Union Springs, was president of the bank in Opelika, Alabama. He knew us and our family. I borrowed $50,000 from the Opelika bank, and that's how I repaid Mr. Mosely, with something left over to help finance the growth of the business!)

We launched our business in May 1946, with Mother owning 20 percent and Houston and me each owning 40 percent. It was a low-budget operation, that's for sure. Our main assets were those four machines, bought on credit. And we ran the company out of the kitchen of Mother's house. One of our first employees was our sister, Barbara, who worked part-time, helping to run the office. I don't remember what we paid her, but I know it wasn't very much.

Although Blount International is known today for having built some of the most complex structures in the world, we began literally at ground level by digging ponds in Bullock County, Alabama. At the time, there was a government program for farmers to build fish ponds to supply water for their cattle. The work was so simple — excavate a hole, erect a small dam and pour a concrete spillway — that even construction greenhorns like Houston and I could handle it with relative ease. Within a few months, we had dug just about all the fish ponds the county could stand. We then began to look for other work, winning a contract to pave some streets and install sewer pipe in Union Springs.

These were great times for the construction industry. In the years following World War II, government at all levels was building roads, bridges and other facilities to modernize and expand the nation's infrastructure. Capitalizing on these opportunities, we increased our revenues rapidly.

There was nothing magic about our early growth. We succeeded for three reasons: we worked hard, we took chances and we hired good people. One of our first employees was Frazier Pair, a soft-spoken family man who had a marvelous talent for operating virtually any kind of machinery. Sitting at the controls of a road-grader,

Frazier could "blue top" a road — that is, smooth its surface to the exact level of the blue tops of stakes that had been placed by highway engineers — as if it were the easiest thing in the world to do. Frazier later managed our equipment yard and stayed with Blount until his death in the 1960s. Another early employee was Sam Wilson, a childhood friend from Union Springs, who had just returned from World War II. Sam was working for a bank in Union Springs and was bored with his job. We convinced him to join us in 1947 as our first full-time office manager. We were lucky to have him. With his personality and wit, Sam is a born optimist and a tenacious go-getter. Soon, he was helping us with estimating and then with sales. Sam stayed with Blount for nearly four decades, retiring in 1984 as vice president in charge of business development. A third early employee was James Griffin. That was our entire staff in 1947: those three employees, Houston and myself.

In those early years, we got to know some influential people in unexpected ways. One of our earliest road-building jobs was in Pike County, Alabama, where we had a subcontract for the base and grading of a six-mile highway. Not being experts in this type of work, we hired an engineer, Leslie Jones, from the state highway department.

This modest edifice in Notasulga, Alabama, was the first building ever constructed by Blount. Just a few years later, we were putting up some of the largest and most complex structures in America.

Leslie and Houston went to Pike County to supervise the project. Local people turned out by the dozens to watch the work, and they kept giving Houston advice. One day, an older, white-haired man was sitting on his haunches, taking in the action. As Houston walked by, this man declared, "Son, if you'd run the tractors around this way and pick up the dirt and go that way, it would be more efficient." Having by now had his fill of advice, Houston snapped back, "Look, old man, if I need your help I'll ask for it." The "old man" turned out to be "Captain" Martin, head of the Bureau of Public Roads for the State of Alabama. That was our introduction to this fine gentleman. Later, as our business grew, we became good friends with "Captain" Martin, and he loved to kid us about that occasion. Houston didn't find it very funny at the time, though.

In 1936, my father bought the short-line Tuskegee Railroad and built this sand and gravel plant on it to help generate traffic. This is one of the plants our family sold to the Ireland family in 1956 when they were putting together a number of businesses to create Vulcan Materials Company.

We were also helped by people who had been friends of our father and thought highly of him. As subcontractors, we were still at the bottom of the construction pecking order. We needed a contractor's license to bid directly on road and bridge work. Therefore, I went to the state licensing board, which was headed by Mr. Quin Flowers, a contractor from Dothan, Alabama. Although the licensing process was complex, Mr. Flowers, who had known our father, took me under his wing, and we got our license in 1947, just one year after starting our company.

We were a couple of brash newcomers to the construction business, ready to take on the world. And we were very aggressive in some of our bids. There was a particular job that included the planting of grass along the side of a road. Even though the bidding terms called for 300,000 square yards of grassing, on close examination I decided the actual amount was much less, so I bid the grass work very low and got the job. The next day, Houston ran into Mr. Vandergriff, whom I mentioned earlier as the fellow who had given me a rough time when I was late with an asphalt delivery in 1941. Mr. Vandergriff was very agitated and asked Houston, "What the hell is Red doing bidding such a low price on all that grassing?" Houston replied, "Well, Mr. Vandergriff, that's just the advantage of a college education." Mr. Vandergriff didn't have a college education, but, in fact, neither did I. Nonetheless, my analysis turned out to be correct and we made money on the contract.

About this same time, I made a deal with three brothers, Oscar, Tom and M. I. Smith, who specialized in small highway bridge projects. They supplied the expertise for us to start building bridges. Soon, with a little experience under our belts, we were bidding on road and bridge work throughout Alabama and Mississippi, winning a number of contracts.

A MEDICAL SCARE

Several months after starting our business, we moved the office out of Mother's home to the second floor of the family-owned railway depot in Tuskegee. I had succeeded my father as president of the short-line Tuskegee Railroad, and it made sense to move to the depot. Not only did we have more space at that location, but it was closer to our family's asphalt and sand and gravel plants. Tuskegee, famous as the home of Booker T. Washington's Tuskegee Institute, was then a small community with only two practicing medical doctors, a point I was soon to discover firsthand.

One day, without warning, I passed out, falling to the floor with a thud. Sam Wilson or Houston, I'm not sure which, immediately called Dr. Yancey. Several minutes later, as he arrived, I was just beginning to regain consciousness. I was only 26 years old and had always enjoyed perfect health. After examining me briefly, Dr. Yancey told Houston to call the other doctor, Dr. Taylor, declaring ominously, "This boy is going out!" Dr. Taylor arrived and decided I had suffered a heart attack. He started pumping me full of a drug — digitalis, I believe. Back on my feet and concerned by what had happened, a few days later I saw a specialist in Birmingham. To my relief, he found there was nothing wrong with my heart — that, in fact, I had collapsed due to exhaustion from working nearly around the clock which was aggravated by a stomach ailment. The specialist recommended that I take a one-month sabbatical, which I did. I have always been a workaholic. But that frightening incident was a warning I have heeded all my life: know my physical limits, and always find time to balance work with pleasure.

Or maybe I'm kidding myself. Recently, I came across an article from the *Montgomery Advertiser*. Written in 1961, 13 years after I had taken my forced sabbatical, it quoted my then-wife, Mary Katherine, as saying, "He puts in an 18-hour day and has been putting off a vacation for two years." She also said, "How many times have I heard, 'Business before pleasure.' Red does not like yard work, PTA, barbecuing, planning entertainment, changing diapers, tonsillectomies, etc." (Guilty as charged.) On the other hand, she acknowledged, "He is a good father. His time is scarce and he gives more of himself in his short time than most men who have more time to spare."

To be closer to the office and cut down on travel, I moved my growing family to a small rented duplex house in Tuskegee. Sam was born in May 1947, joining Winton, three years old, and Tommy, not quite two. Kay and Joe would follow in the 1950s after we had moved to Montgomery.

As the head of a small, thriving business, I was constantly on the go, crisscrossing Alabama and Mississippi to bid on work and supervise jobs. I drove a gold Buick with large fins. The ride was comfortable, but the car itself was quite flashy. No one else in Tuskegee owned one like it, nor did they seem to want to. Neighbors sometimes looked out their windows to watch me come and go at all hours of the early morning and late at night. In 1948, to reduce my travel time further, I bought a single-engine Navion airplane which I piloted to job sites. It was the first of many airplanes I would own over the years. (Later, when our company bought its first twin-engine plane, we had our pilots take flight safety training twice a year, and I took it with them. I flew regularly until 1981, when I reached the company retirement age for pilots. I have missed it ever since.)

Tuskegee was typical of many small southern cities in that people were very sociable and liked to get together. A group of younger couples started a club in an old house outside town, and every Friday night we would all go there and turn on the nickelodeon and dance and have a great time. Even though I was exhausted from having worked hard all week, I wanted to be a party person, too. Sometimes I would arrive at the club and dance a little, then sneak off to a corner and go to sleep. When roused by the other men, I would wake up saying to no one in particular, "I don't want to go home. I don't want to go home."

MY BROTHER LEAVES THE COMPANY

Houston was a key player in our company's early growth. But he did not stay long. In 1948, he left Blount Brothers Construction Company to join our uncle, Colonel Roberts Blount, in his businesses. Houston was to be gone "temporarily." Or so we both thought.

Uncle Roberts lived in Tallassee, about 40 miles north of Union Springs. Like his brother (our father), he was a successful entrepreneur, owning two sand and gravel plants and three concrete pipe plants. However, he had no children to succeed him, and several times he had said to us, "One of you ought to come over here and ultimately take over my businesses." Houston and I talked about that, and Houston finally decided to go. A few years later, when Uncle Roberts retired, Houston and I bought his businesses. About two years after that, in 1956, Charles Ireland, whose family owned Birmingham Slag Company, approached us about acquiring these businesses to merge with a group of companies the Irelands were planning to take public. We owned a plant with the Irelands that made concrete pipe, so we knew them quite well and thought highly of them. We agreed to their offer, receiving stock in the new company, Vulcan Materials, which subsequently listed its shares on the New York Stock Exchange and is today one of the major industrial corporations in the South and a leading world producer of aggregates.

At the invitation of the Irelands, Houston joined Vulcan at its inception in 1956 to get its concrete pipe division off the ground. Two years later, it had been nearly a decade since Houston had left Blount Brothers Construction Company "temporarily." We both agreed the time had come for him to make a decision — either to stay with Vulcan or return to Blount. He decided on the former, and we worked out a deal in which he received my share of the Vulcan stock in return for my receiving his share of Blount Brothers Construction Company. (At about the same time, I bought Mother's interest in Blount Brothers Construction Company for around $300,000, providing her with a nest egg on which she lived comfortably the rest of her life. As a result, by the late 1950s I was the company's sole owner.)

The deal with Houston was friendly, and he stayed on the board of directors of Blount — and remains a board member to this day. He has consistently been one of our most active directors and has always been someone I have turned to for advice regarding the company. Houston went on to become chief executive officer of Vulcan Materials in the 1980s. I'm very proud of him. We've both had great careers.

FIRST AVENUE VIADUCT: PIVOTAL PROJECT FOR BLOUNT

Whenever I recount the early years of Blount, there is one project I always relish talking about: the First Avenue Viaduct in Birmingham. It was our first $1 million contract. We undertook it just three years after starting the company, which shows how rapidly we had progressed from digging fish ponds in Bullock County. We constructed the viaduct — a six-lane bridge with provisions built in for streetcar tracks — in 1949. It's still there, and it represents a landmark in the history of the company because of its size and the lessons we learned from it.

Many contractors were skeptical about our ability to take on

PROPOSED
FEDERAL AID PROJECT U.G.I. 280(3)

FIRST AVENUE VIADUCT

BIRMINGHAM, ALABAMA

TO REPLACE PRESENT STRUCTURE EXTENDING FROM
26th STREET TO 31st STREET

DESIGNED FOR

ALABAMA STATE HIGHWAY DEPARTMENT
BY
POLK, POWELL & HENDON
ENGINEERS
BIRMINGHAM, ALABAMA

WIDTH	ROADWAY——6 TRAFFIC LANES	73 FEET
	TOTAL STRUCTURE	83 FEET
LENGTH	FROM 25th STREET TO 35th STREET	
	WEST APPROACH	828.64 FEET
	OPEN BRIDGE STRUCTURE	2,953.74 FEET
	EAST APPROACH	1,072.59 FEET
	TOTAL PROJECT	4,854.97 FEET

The First Avenue Viaduct, completed in 1949 in Birmingham, was Blount's first $1 million project. Other contractors insisted our bid was far too low and advised me to default the contract rather than build the viaduct at a loss. I disagreed, and in fact, we ended up making a nice profit.

such a project. They questioned our experience and said our bid was too low to make a profit. (To visualize just how low it was, I took the difference between our bid and the next-lowest bid and converted the amount to bottles of Jim Beam bourbon — 14,588 bottles, I reckoned. I could see all of those bottles in my mind, and that's when I realized how low we were. Those bottles would have kept me in bourbon the rest of my life!) Several contractors advised me to default our $10,000 bid bond and walk away from the project, rather than risk getting in over our heads. To which I replied, "We bid the job to get it, and I think we can do it at that price." As in previous projects, I thought the key was to hire the right people. I therefore looked for an experienced construction man to run the project and found Mr. C. C. Davis, who had supervised the building of Martin Dam in the 1920s on the Tallapoosa River for Hardaway Contracting Company. Coincidentally, Hardaway was the same company that had built the first six miles of my grandfather's railroad around the turn of the century. With his quiet self-confidence and experience in large projects, Mr. Davis was a wonderful addition to our company.

The viaduct project was, in fact, a big risk for Blount. I had bid low by basing my cost estimates on the idea of using nonunion labor, even though Birmingham was a union town. On the other hand, I am adamant in my belief that problems should be dealt with head-on. So after hiring Mr. Davis, I arranged for the two of us to meet with the leaders of the Birmingham construction unions at the Redmont Hotel on a Sunday afternoon. We told them of our plan and, of course, they objected. I also recognized there had to be some give on my part. So after a rather animated discussion, we reached a compromise that all our foremen would be nonunion but the rest of the construction crew would be union.

I thought the matter was settled — until someone blew up one of our cranes with dynamite in the middle of the night. To me, it was obvious the unions were delivering a message that they would not accept the use of nonunion foremen, after all. We called the police, but they were friendly with the unions and made absolutely no effort to solve the crime. So I said to Mr. Davis, "We're going to the union headquarters," to which he replied, "We can't do that, it's too dangerous." But we went anyway and, I guarantee you, we were very much on edge as we walked into the building, down a hallway and into the union office. About a dozen union executives and members were inside. It would be an understatement to say they were surprised to see us. I had quite a temper in those days. Entering that room, I immediately took the offensive and said, "Look, I know damn well that every one of you knows who blew up that crane. I want to tell you, we're going to put armed guards on this project with orders to shoot to kill. And you'd better stop this violence or someone's going to get hurt." A few heated words ensued, and we left. It was a long walk out of the office and back down that hallway. However, our visit paid off. There was no further trouble.

Shortly before construction of the viaduct began, I happened to read a magazine article which said that Andrew Carnegie used to show up unannounced at his steel mills and write numbers on the floor with chalk. He then left without explanation. It was not long before his workers realized that the numbers represented the tons of steel produced by each shift each day. This awareness gave each shift an incentive to want to be the best and outperform the others. In this manner, productivity was improved.

I thought, why not have an incentive program for the viaduct? So I divided the crew into two teams, the North team and the South team, and announced I would give a turkey to each member of the team that had built the most concrete spans by Thanksgiving. Each day, I wrote the latest results on a blackboard by the entrance to the construction site. When Thanksgiving arrived, I handed out nearly 50 turkeys to the members of the winning team. Pleased with the other team's efforts, too, I gave my friend John Overton, our bonding agent, some cash and told him to buy them 50 chickens. The turkeys and chickens may not have been the only factor in the project's success, but we did finish three months ahead of schedule and under budget. Blount Brothers Construction Company earned a nice profit.

My bonus turkeys marked the beginning of our incentive programs at Blount. Today, of course, they are much more sophisticated and financially rewarding. But we have always used incentives as a way to improve performance, going right back to 1949.

When the First Avenue Viaduct was completed, and before it was opened to traffic, I invited a few of my friends to a celebration. We sat on that bridge at night, under the stars, and enjoyed a few drinks, toasting the pleasures of life.

It has now been many years since we built the First Avenue Viaduct, but it still holds a special place in my heart.

THE IMPORTANCE OF A STRONG RELATIONSHIP WITH A BONDING COMPANY

Bonding is a fundamental requirement for any construction company. Every contractor needs to obtain two types of bonds: a bid bond to guarantee that the company will sign the contract if it submits the winning bid, and a performance bond to guarantee the timely completion of the project according to specifications. Having a strong relationship with a bonding company is vital to a contractor's success.

In the late 1940s, when we began bidding on highway jobs in Mississippi, at one letting we won four jobs totaling $1 million. We obtained our bonding for those jobs through two brokers named Bottrell and Fields. Shortly thereafter, I had a telephone call from Dan Bottrell who said he and Fields were coming through Tuskegee on their way to Atlanta and wanted to drop by to see me. We were living in a duplex apartment, not very fancy to say the least. I invited them over for dinner. Following the meal, we had a few drinks and began to chat when one of them suddenly asked, "Red, how old are you?" Curious as to what they were getting at, I said, "How old do you think I am?" To which one of them replied, "We know you were a pilot in the war, and we think you're probably 32." I remarked that they had missed by seven years, prompting the question, "You mean you're 39?" "Oh no," I replied, "I'm 25." You could see their jaws drop. Fields turned to Bottrell and exclaimed, "Dan, we're bonding a couple of BOYS!" But they kept supporting us. Somehow, Houston and I gave them the confidence to do so.

Our bonding broker in Alabama was John Overton. Initially, he placed our coverage with National Surety Company. However, National got cold feet when we were low bidder on the First Avenue Viaduct. Apparently, they felt we were biting off more than we could chew, and they did not want to assume the risk. A fellow from National said to me, "Red, you've got to decide whether you're going to be in the railroad business or the contracting business" — and with those words, they kissed us off. Their decision, however, ended up costing them a ton of money, because John Overton then switched our account to the United States Fidelity & Guaranty Company, which stuck with us for decades through bigger and bigger projects. John and USF&G were keys to our ability to grow.

John Overton, My Best Friend

Let me tell you about John Overton. John, a truly fabulous character, died in 1981. He was the best friend I ever had.

John worked his way through Auburn University waiting on tables and graduated with a degree in agriculture. During World War II, when he was exempt from military service for medical reasons, he worked initially for the government buying chickens (which is why I asked him to buy the chickens for the losing team on the First Avenue Viaduct). One day during the war, John happened to meet

John Overton was the best friend I ever had. He and his wife, Vesta Lou, didn't have any children, and their dog was like a surrogate child. It was a very friendly pooch. One time, I was walking along a street in downtown Montgomery with John, the dog and Alabama Governor "Big Jim" Folsom. John was greatly amused that everybody we passed said hello to the dog, but nobody said a word to the three of us.

Tilghman Turner, owner of Turner Insurance & Bonding Company in Montgomery. Mr. Turner immediately recognized that John was a natural-born salesman and hired him.

Mr. Turner went to North Alabama for a week to see his mother shortly after hiring John. As the contractors came in during that week, John, being new to the business, signed their bonds left and right without bothering to look at what he was signing. When Mr. Turner returned, the office was in chaos. A few days later, Mr. Turner was playing checkers with his cousin, Paul Turner, by an open window in the office. A football game was being played that night in Montgomery, and somebody threw a roll of toilet paper off the top of the Bell Building. As the toilet paper unwound and fluttered by the open window, Mr. Turner said to his cousin, "Paul, close that window quick, cause if that stuff floats in here John will sure as hell sign it."

I first met John shortly before Christmas 1946 at the Whitley Hotel in Montgomery, where all the contractors had gathered in preparation for a public works contract letting. John was there to offer bonding. We quickly struck up a friendship.

John was a huge man, over 300 pounds. He could be slovenly and loud. But you just had to love him. He was the most enthusiastic person I have ever known. And he had absolute confidence in me. As our company grew and needed larger amounts of bonding, he never failed to deliver.

John used to fly with me on business all over the country. I'd phone on the spur of the moment and say, "Let's go to Omaha," and he would show up at the airport, raring to get started. One time we were in Chicago. I finished my meetings late in the afternoon and we headed back to Montgomery in my single-engine Beechcraft

We bought our first corporate plane in the late 1940s so I could fly to job sites across Alabama and Mississippi. By the early 1960s, we had graduated to this World War II Lockheed Ventura, remodeled for corporate use. That's me about to enter the aircraft. Jim Perkins, our company pilot, is by the side of the airplane next to the tail, with his head leaning forward.

Bonanza, just the two of us, with me at the controls. By 8 p.m., when we were over Nashville, I informed John that we were running low on fuel but I would try to make Birmingham — and, if we couldn't get that far, I would stop at Huntsville, which was halfway. By the time we crossed the Alabama border and were nearing Huntsville, the fuel gauge was close to empty. I tried to raise the Huntsville airport for permission to land, but could not get an answer. Finally, I reached an area control network, and they told me the Huntsville airport had closed for the night. I said, "John, it looks like we're going to have to make Birmingham after all." John tried his best to remain calm and cheerful, but you could just see his nerves unraveling. We ultimately reached Birmingham and landed without incident, although moments after touching down the plane ran out of fuel and we had to be towed to a hangar. On reaching that hangar, John got out of our Beechcraft Bonanza airplane, flashed his credit card and said, "Fill up this plane with fuel and run it over on the ground." Thereafter, every time John traveled with me on my plane, he would pay for the fuel — and make sure the tanks were filled to capacity. In the 1960s, I bought a much larger airplane, a Lockheed Ventura that had been converted after the war to carry up to 12 passengers. On our first trip in that plane, John and I and three or four others flew to Baltimore to visit with the USF&G, our bonding company. Upon landing at the Baltimore airport, John, as usual, pulled out his credit card and said, "Fill 'er up." We then went into the city for our meetings and returned to the airport the next day for the trip back to Montgomery. At this point, John collected his receipt. It was for something like 1,500 gallons of aviation fuel and an enormous amount of oil. Believe me, that was the last time John Overton ever offered to buy fuel for my airplane.

I miss flying. I have given up my pilot's license now that I am in my 70s.

With his huge size, John was an unforgettable sight on a horse. One time, John, Houston, Barney Monaghan (of our law firm, Bradley Arant) and I were hunting near the little town of Midway, Alabama, when John's horse stepped in a hole, throwing him over its head. John was knocked out cold on impact with the ground. The best that Barney, a Rhodes scholar, could do was keep repeating, "Don't go, John, don't go." We borrowed a truck and drove John to St. Margaret's Hospital in Montgomery, where it was discovered he had a broken vertebra in his neck. The next day, I hurt my knee getting on a horse and ended up in the same hospital. My family had a round-about relationship with the hospital: Uncle Bob's wife, who was born a South Alabama Baptist, was converted to Catholicism by Monsignor Fulton Sheen, later Bishop Sheen of TV fame. To honor his wife's conversion, Uncle Bob built a little jewel of a Catholic church in Tallassee, and Catholics from all over Alabama came to the consecration. When I checked into St. Margaret's, I guess the nuns recognized my name. They must have, because they assigned me to the lavish Bishop's Room, complete with four-poster bed. Hearing I was in the same hospital, John, now recovering, paid me a visit. He was dumbfounded when he came into that room, wondering how in the world I had the clout to get such magnificent digs. I can still hear him complaining loudly that my bathroom alone was bigger than his entire room. And it was!

John had a heart as big as his girth. And he believed he could do anything in the world — which he could. He used to remark, "Red, if they don't say yes to us, that's because we haven't talked to them long enough."

In 1950, I mentioned to John that road contracting was a tough way to make a living. And he replied, "Why don't you build buildings?" I said I didn't know anything about that line of business. The biggest contractor in the South at that time was Daniels Construction Company, based in Greenville, South Carolina. John was close to the Daniels people and he said, "Red, I guarantee that you are just as smart as they are." His comments inspired me. I decided we were ready to move up to the big leagues and compete with the major contractors for large building projects.

CHAPTER THREE

Hiring a Winner

In 1950, WE MOVED OUR OFFICE TO MONT-gomery — a larger base from which to develop Blount into a national company — and won our first contracts to build a couple of small gymnasiums and remodel a bank. Because I was a business manager who happened to be in the construction business, not a construction specialist, I knew we needed someone with expertise if we were to compete for contracts to put up large structures. I therefore began a national search for the right person. It was through an advertisement I placed in the *Wall Street Journal* that we found Paul Hess.

Paul, some 20 years my senior, was a tough-minded construction executive in the prime of his career. A graduate of MIT, he had been involved in the building of huge complexes such as Rockefeller Center and the Chicago Merchandise Mart. At the time he responded to our ad, he was a vice president of Barlow-Meagher Co., a major New York City contracting firm. Paul was well settled in New York, where he had lived all his life. I doubt that he ever would have left except that his wife, known as "T," developed a respiratory ailment and doctors advised her to move to a warmer climate. So it was a matter of happenstance that a tremendously capable executive, who fit our particular requirements, was available just when we needed him.

Beginning in 1951, I wooed Paul for nearly five months before convincing him to come on board. First, having received his letter in response to our ad, I asked my brother Houston to interview him on a

Opposite, launch pad 37 at Cape Canaveral was one of the many large facilities built by Blount beginning in the 1950s. Our strategy was to specialize in complex, fixed-price projects. Although they were riskier than routine brick-and-mortar assignments, the profit potential was much greater. Left, Paul Hess led our building division for nearly 20 years. Hiring Paul was one of the best decisions I ever made.

visit Houston was planning to New York. They met at the Waldorf-Astoria Hotel, and Houston reported back favorably. I then invited Paul and his wife to Montgomery, where we spent a day with them, getting to know them both. Paul was one of several people we interviewed, and when I got through his abrasive personality, he was far and away the most impressive. That very day, before he and his wife left Montgomery, I offered him a job. From Montgomery, Paul was heading west to Santa Fe for an interview with another company, and he said he would get back to me, which he eventually did, accepting my offer in September 1951. Incidentally, Paul, a Yankee from the word go, soon succumbed to the charms of the South and could no longer understand why anyone would live in New York.

With the enlistment of Paul Hess to head our building division, Blount embarked on a period of spectacular growth. Paul deserves a great deal of the credit for this success. Paul began at a salary of $25,000, with substantial performance incentives on top of that. My salary was $15,000. When a close friend asked why I would pay Paul more than I paid myself, I replied, "Because he's a winner."

Paul Hess and his wife, "T," were dyed-in-the-wool New Yorkers who came to Montgomery after "T" developed a respiratory ailment and had to move to a warmer climate.

And, indeed, he was. There was nothing special about Paul in terms of physical appearance. Of German ancestry, he was short and bald and was an undistinguished dresser. He smoked cigarettes in moderation and enjoyed an occasional cigar. What set him apart were his astuteness and unique personality. Nothing ever escaped Paul's steel-trap mind. At the same time, he had an abrupt, even confrontational manner that tended to keep employees off-balance. Small talk did not interest him in the least. If someone mentioned it was a nice day, he might respond, "Why?" and not say another word. He could also be a tough taskmaster. John Caddell, who joined us in 1952, tells the story of a young engineer hired by Paul in the 1950s. When the engineer reported to work the first day, Paul didn't immediately have anything for him to do, so he asked the fellow to recalculate some figures; it was pure make-work. The engineer understood the nature of what Paul had asked him to do and made the mistake of saying, "Gee, Mr. Hess, if you don't have any work for me right now, that's okay." Paul fired the fellow on the spot. Less than two hours after this engineer had joined the company, he was out the door. Paul was simply put off by that response.

What Paul lacked in charm he made up for in performance. For nearly two decades under his leadership, from 1952 to 1969, our building division never lost money on a major project — a remarkable achievement in the construction industry. There are two keys to success in construction. One is to *bid* a profitable job. The other is to *build* a job profitably. All the rest is fluff. Paul was very good at estimating costs in order to bid a price that was competitive yet offered room for profit. And when it came to the second part of the equation — building a job profitably, that is, completing it to specifications at or under budget — he was an absolute master.

In any fixed-price construction contract, there are hundreds or even thousands of individual line items that have been added up to arrive at the total price. Each of these items is a potential booby trap: if any item goes significantly over budget during construction, the entire project may lose money. That is one reason why the construction business is so volatile and why so few firms survive for an extended period; a bad cost overrun on just one item can be fatal. Paul was relentless in monitoring each project and controlling costs. He visited each construction site periodically, meeting with the superintendent and other managers and grilling them to the nth degree about the status of actual costs versus budgeted costs, item by item. Within our company, this grueling process came to be known as "the Hess inquisition."

Years later, I heard Larry Appley of the American Management Association proclaim that people will do what management inspects, not what it expects. That captures Paul's philosophy in a nutshell, even if he didn't express it that way himself.

Despite his gruff personality, Paul and I got along well and made a good team — and teamwork is very powerful in business. My role was to set the strategic direction; motivate people; take the lead in marketing; handle all financial matters, such as bank relationships and bonding; and be a high-level trouble-shooter. Paul's role, equally vital, was to manage the building division. I gave him free rein to do so, subject to accountability for results. At the same time, understanding the importance of keeping me informed, Paul never failed to come to me when a problem arose. He would call me wherever I was, whatever I was doing, if there was something that needed my attention. We trusted each other completely, and that is one reason we worked well together.

Looking back over the past 50 years, this is the pattern of the way I have managed — hire highly qualified specialists and form a tightly knit team in which everybody is up-front with each other; nothing is held back.

Construction is a very challenging business. At the risk of offending my friends in manufacturing, let me suggest that running a manufacturing company is a piece of cake compared to running a construction company. One of the key differences is this:

In manufacturing, you open a factory and keep producing at that same location with essentially the same management and employees year after year. And you can train those employees to meet your quality and productivity standards.

Construction, by contrast, is one of the few businesses where your product and workforce keep changing. You win a contract, hire construction workers from a local pool, complete the project in two or three years and then move on to the next job at a different location, hiring a new group of managers and workers.

Because there is so little continuity from one construction project to the next, it is imperative to have a solid core of full-time management and support staff. These people are the heart and soul of any construction company.

Shortly after Paul Hess joined us, we began to staff up by recruiting young engineers from nearly two dozen colleges — Georgia Tech, Auburn, the University of Alabama, the University of Tennessee, the University of Florida and others. We hired approximately 20 a year, putting each newcomer through a rigorous training program, beginning with a year in the estimating department followed by stints in other departments, such as contract management, as well as giving them experience in the field. In this way, we developed an exceptional staff with a well-rounded view of the company. A very significant addition was John Caddell out of Georgia Tech in 1952. John was destined to play a huge role in our growth and success as a major construction company.

Paul worked closely with these recruits and became their mentor. This was surprising to me, given his brusque personality. Yet, he seemed to savor the role of coach and teacher. He spent many hours with these young engineers sharing his insights about the construction business. He bonded with them and inspired them and demanded performance. And nearly every day he would invite a group of them to lunch to discuss problems and offer advice. But he always made everyone at the table gamble as to who would pay for lunch. Paul seldom lost.

To add experience to our staff, we hired several veterans of the construction industry, such as Charlie Jones, Jr., who came to us from a company in the Carolinas. Later, Charlie's son and grandson worked for Blount. Others included Bill Mullins, who had been a field engineer on major projects in Texas; Carl Wiggs, who had worked for the Tennessee Valley Authority and the U.S. Corps of Engineers; Nolan West, who joined us from a construction company in Mobile, Alabama; Jim Satterwhite; and Charlie Smith.

Another key addition was Holman Head, who became my administrative assistant in the late 1950s. He was enormously helpful to me, particularly in civic work and other outside activities, drafting speeches and in areas related to company policy and organization. He went to Washington with me in 1969 when I joined the Nixon administration, returned to Alabama in 1972 and rejoined Blount in 1974. He stayed with Blount until 1979, when he left to become executive director of the Alabama Chamber of Commerce.

A KEY STRATEGIC DECISION: FOCUS ON COMPLEX PROJECTS

In 1952, our newly formed building division won its first three major contracts, including this atomic energy plant at Oak Ridge, Tennessee. Our success in completing these early projects on time and within budget gave us the confidence to specialize in large, fixed-price contracts.

In 1952, our newly formed building division got off to a robust start by winning three major contracts. One was an assignment to construct a radar and electronics building and flight operations hangar for Lockheed Aircraft in Marietta, Georgia. The other two, with a higher degree of complexity, were a $700,000 contract to build a small

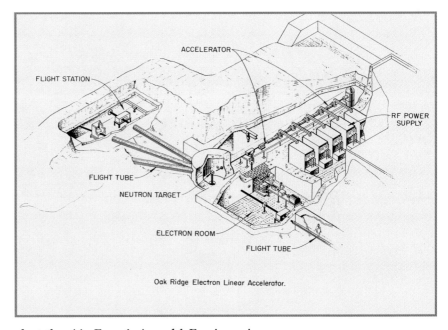

Oak Ridge Electron Linear Accelerator.

portion of a wind tunnel at the Air Force's Arnold Engineering Development Center in Tullahoma, Tennessee, and a $2.7 million contract to build the first atomic energy plant ever let by the government on a fixed-price basis. Those dollar amounts may sound small. But remember, they were 1952 dollars and were substantial at that time. The atomic energy plant was in Oak Ridge, Tennessee. At the beginning of that job, I got a phone call from Paul Hess, who was in Oak Ridge supervising the initial stages of the project. He had not yet fully adjusted to living and working in the South. He exclaimed,

"Red, we've got this job to do up here, but how do I find the hunkies?" I said, "Paul, what in the world are you talking about? I never heard of hunkies." And he replied, "In New York, if you get a construction project and you want to start building forms and pouring concrete, you call the hunkies and they do it for you." I said, "Paul, we're not in New York. We've got to do that ourselves."

All three jobs that we won in 1952 were completed on time and within budget. And this success gave us confidence to make a major strategic decision: we would specialize in complex projects. Such ventures are riskier than routine assignments. On the other hand, the profit potential is greater because there are fewer competitors. We escalated our risk by focusing on fixed-price contracts, as opposed to cost-plus jobs. Again, we did this because of superior profit potential. We simply felt we could tackle complicated jobs better than most of our competitors by utilizing the brains and abilities of our people to analyze and manage them exceptionally well.

Our strategy worked. One-of-a-kind and first-of-a-kind projects became the hallmark of Blount. In the ensuing years, we built some of the most exciting projects of our time.

Opposite, another of our major 1952 projects was this radar and electronics building and flight operations hangar for Lockheed Aircraft in Marietta, Georgia. Right, during the 1950s we expanded our staff, adding many experienced construction people, including Charlie Smith (in the front row, holding his hard hat).

An early landmark project was the nation's first Atlas intercontinental missile base, which we constructed in 1958 near Cheyenne, Wyoming. This facility was built in response to Sputnik and the escalating tensions of the Cold War. In August 1957, when Premier Khrushchev announced that the Soviet Union had tested "a super long-distance intercontinental multi-stage ballistic missile," the first of its kind, few Americans paid any attention. Two months later, however, the Russians stunned the world by putting Sputnik into orbit around the earth. Russia had not only beaten America into space but had also made good on Khrushchev's claim of leadership in long-range missilery. Young people today may not realize just how shocking Sputnik was. In one dramatic action, the Soviets had challenged

In the late 1950s, to counter Soviet advances in long-range missilery, America began building a series of bases housing intercontinental ballistic missiles. We were chosen to build the first of these facilities, pictured here, near Cheyenne, Wyoming.

John Overton, Paul Hess and I posed at a contract-signing for the Cheyenne project.

our belief in America's military superiority and had demonstrated that it possessed long-range missiles that might be used to deliver nuclear warheads. To counter the Soviet threat, the United States immediately began building a series of intercontinental missile bases. Blount was chosen to build the first, near Cheyenne — an indication of just how far we had come as a company from our origins of digging fish ponds in rural Alabama. Because the missile program was brand-new and was being developed on a crash basis, the Cheyenne project involved some unprecedented technical challenges, including a requirement that we maintain hospital-type cleanliness at the construction site (to 10,000ths of a micron, the first time this standard had ever been applied in such circumstances) and the welding of metals to other metals that had never before been welded together. To make matters even more complicated, the design specifications for the base kept changing: every time a ballistic missile was launched from Cape Canaveral in Florida, the specifications for the base were revised to incorporate the latest findings. The project turned out to be a formidable challenge, but our people rose to the occasion and got the job done.

Other important projects included:
• A massive indoor "ocean" to test ship designs for the U.S. Navy at Carderock, Maryland — a structure so large and technically complex that we had to take into account the curvature of the earth when building it.
• Launch pads across the country for the Mercury, Gemini and Apollo programs, including Cape Canaveral's launch complex 39A, from which Neil Armstrong's historic trip to the moon lifted off in 1969.
• A huge space environment simulator at Sandusky, Ohio, used to test-fire nuclear engines in a vacuum, as they would be used in space.
• The New Orleans Superdome, the largest structure of its kind in the world when it was completed in 1975.
• The magnificent PPG World Headquarters in Pittsburgh, Pennsylvania, a 60-story Gothic office building that resembles a turreted glass palace.

In the 1960s, we built this huge space environment simulator in Sandusky, Ohio, for use in test-firing nuclear engines in outer-space-like conditions.

The contribution of these and other projects to revenues was astounding. Versus contracts of $350,000 in 1947, our first full year, active contracts surged to $100 million by February 1962, shortly after I had reached the ripe old age of 40. And we kept right on growing throughout the remainder of the 1960s, '70s and '80s.

Some of Blount's most distinctive projects from its
peak years in construction
include launch complex
39A at Cape Canaveral,
from which the Apollo 11
astronauts lifted off for the
moon; the magnificent,
glass-sheathed PPG
Industries headquarters,
designed by Philip Johnson
in the style of a Gothic
tower, in downtown
Pittsburgh; and the
Louisiana Superdome in
New Orleans. Huber Hunt
& Nichols was our partner
in the Superdome project.

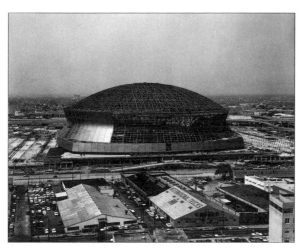

LIVING IN STYLE

In 1956 I was named one of four Outstanding Young Men in Alabama. My Georgian-style home, Wynfield, below, was completed in 1964 on the outskirts of Montgomery. I wanted a beautiful, distinctive house where I could entertain clients, but I also wanted it to be livable, and it has been just that.

My personal life was also moving along at quite a clip. In 1956, I was named one of four Outstanding Young Men in Alabama. Three years later, I was elected to the board of trustees of the University of Alabama, serving for the next 32 years. And in 1961, I was elected president of the Alabama Chamber of Commerce.

Because I wanted a home where we could entertain clients with flair, in 1964 my wife and I completed our Georgian-style house, Wynfield, on the outskirts of Montgomery. (People are sometimes confused, and understandably so, because my first name is Winton, spelled with an "i," but my home, Wynfield, and the Wynton M. Blount Cultural Park in Montgomery are both spelled with a "y." In this regard, I follow the practice of my father, whose first name on his birth certificate was Wynton, as is mine, but who used Winton in public life to avoid having to explain constantly the spelling of his name.) Wynfield was designed by Mott Schmidt, the preeminent Georgian architect in the country at that time. The original concept was to have a beautiful, distinctive house to support the business, but I also wanted it to be livable, and for more than 30 years it has been just that.

Right, in 1989 Carolyn and I bought this vacation home in Beaver Creek, Colorado. A ski run begins right outside our back door. How's that for convenience?

Aubrey Dubose, our house manager for more than 10 years, has helped make life comfortable not only for Carolyn and me but also for our guests, handling his duties with grace and warmth.

John Lesenger

Someone else who has been very important in making Wynfield livable is John Lesenger, our estate manager, who came to work for me 20 years ago. John is a delightful Scotsman who had apprenticed in Scotland and England before managing Stonecrop, an estate in Cold Spring, New York. He is an accomplished landscape gardener who has been a tremendous asset as we have developed the grounds around Wynfield. We have also encouraged him to get involved with garden clubs in the Montgomery area, and he is in great demand as a speaker. John is indefatigable and seldom says no. He is a leader of the local Scottish Society and plays the big drum in its bagpipe band. When he carries that drum, you can barely see the top of his head.

John Lesenger has been with me 20 years as gillie of Wynfield. With his pride in his work and his dedication to the highest standards, combined with his delightfully biting sense of humor, John is an extraordinary individual.

John is responsible for our grounds, managing the landscaping workforce and all equipment. His title used to be superintendent of Wynfield. However, when Carolyn and I went to Scotland a couple of years ago, we found that a person with the same responsibilities on a Scottish estate is called a gillie, a title of distinction. I came back and told John he was now the gillie of Wynfield. He readily agreed.

Despite his 25 years in the United States, John has lost very little of his Scottish brogue. When he and I get together for a conference, I always listen intently. But when he stops, I inevitably turn to Carolyn and ask, "What did he say?" even when I have my hearing aid in.

Good times at Lake Martin

Beginning in the 1950s, I also owned a vacation cottage at Lake Martin, northeast of Montgomery. It was there that my family had some wonderful times together, including sailing expeditions on an unusual vessel I had acquired on a whim. In the late 1950s, I was at a business meeting in Hawaii and decided to return home the long way, across Asia and Europe. One of my friends, Henry Kotkins from Seattle, planned a similar trip, so we agreed to meet in Hong Kong. Henry, an avid sailor, was having a Chinese junk constructed in the British crown colony. Visiting the shipyard with him, I said on the

My Chinese junk, with its bright orange sails, was an unusual sight in the heart of Dixie. I kept the junk for nearly 10 years, sailing it on Lake Martin northeast of Montgomery. When I left for Washington to join the Nixon cabinet, I gave the junk to the local sailing club, but they gave it right back. On my return from government service, it had rotted beyond repair.

spur of the moment, "I'd like to have one of those too," and they built one for me exactly like his. My junk was shipped from Hong Kong to Mobile by freighter, then trucked to Lake Martin, where we launched her on a blustery March afternoon. With her distinctive lines and bright orange sail, she was quite a sight in the heart of Dixie, invariably attracting a small armada of curious onlookers in motorboats whenever we set sail.

Montgomery is home to the Air War College, the ultimate school of the U.S. Air Force. It includes the Allied Officers School, where officers from all over the world come to train for a year. Citizens in Montgomery "adopt" these overseas students and introduce them to American life. One year, I adopted two allied officers from Cambodia and one from Vietnam. All three loved to join me on the junk. They would put on brief bathing suits and coolie hats, just waiting for the motorboats to circle us. As the boats came within

earshot of the junk, those three officers from the Far East would start saying in broken English, "Mr. Blount, he got junk and me for $25," which was enough to send the motorboats away with the occupants shaking their heads.

Unfortunately, my talent as a sailor did not match my appetite for the acquisition of this exotic vessel. I didn't even know the difference between a jib and a jibe. To make matters worse, the instructions that came with the junk were in Chinese! So it was always quite an adventure whenever I raised sail and set forth with friends and family. On one occasion, I was attempting an especially tricky maneuver when Jeff Samuels, a youngster who was a friend of my son Sam, fell overboard. I happened to be on that side of the boat and reached right down and scooped him back in like an eagle plucking a fish from water. It was a scary moment. If I hadn't grabbed Jeff, he might well have drowned.

Although I loved cruising Lake Martin in my junk, I found it increasingly difficult to enlist my friends to crew. Sailing just once on that boat with Captain Blount at the helm seemed enough for anybody. I kept my junk for nearly 10 years until 1969, when I went to Washington to join the Nixon cabinet. At that time, I gave her to the local sailing club. They couldn't find any use for her, so they promptly gave her back. She was put into storage. When I returned from Washington, she had rotted beyond repair.

MOTHER GOES TO WASHINGTON

Coincidentally, as my personal life flourished, so did my mother's. In the early 1950s, George Andrews, the Congressman I talked about earlier who was a friend of our family, was still serving in the House. He asked Mother to come to Washington to supervise his office. Mother was intelligent and capable, and she welcomed the opportunity. Houston, my sister Barbara and I had all moved from Union Springs. In explaining her decision to take the job, Mother told me, "You know, Son, I get up every morning and go out and touch every camellia bush. And what else have I got to do?" She quickly learned to love Washington, with its hustle and bustle and sophisticated social life. In those days, Congress was in session only six months a year. As a result, she was still able to spend half the year in Alabama with loved ones and friends.

Every time I went to Washington, I took her out to dinner. I looked older than I was, and people who knew my mother but had not previously met me would sometimes ask her, "Is that your brother?" She always got a kick out of that. On one occasion, Mother and I were having dinner at the restaurant on top of the Washington Hotel. I saw some of my friends from New York at a table across the room, and when they had finished their meal, they came over to speak to me and I introduced them to Mother. They all looked at me skeptically and rolled their eyes and said, "Your Mother, huh."

Mother retired in the mid-1960s, and until her death in 1968, she remained one of my closest confidants. I talked with her often about the business, keeping her up to date, which she enjoyed very much. She was very proud of the things I had done but was quick to disagree with me when I told her in the 1960s I was thinking of running for governor of Alabama. Partly at her urging, I did not run. She was a wise lady.

My mother, Clara Belle Chalker Blount, and I were very close. I often turned to her for advice when I was facing difficult business decisions.

I am sometimes asked how I felt during those early years of breakneck expansion for our company. Was I surprised we had succeeded so quickly? Did I have any inkling of what Blount might become? To be honest, I didn't have time to contemplate such matters. I was just working my head off trying to make the company grow as quickly as possible.

But there did come an occasion, on an airplane flight one night in the late 1950s, when I wrote down my business beliefs on the back of an envelope. With very little change, those handwritten notes became the Blount Philosophy, which has guided our company ever since. The Blount Philosophy embraces people as the heart of our company and emphasizes that we will seek to create a climate where individuals can develop to their maximum potential. And it encourages our employees to look beyond their jobs and contribute to society through civic, cultural, religious and political activities.

The Blount Philosophy is something I have lived, day in and day out, since the company's very beginning. In fact, by the late 1950s I had already gained a reputation as an oddity in the business world: someone who spent as much time on political, educational and civic endeavors as I did running my company. There were periods when I would be away from Blount three or four months at a time helping to manage a political campaign — such as the Nixon presidential campaign in 1960, when I was in charge of eight southeastern states — while keeping in touch with the office by phone. (Recently, our receptionist, Cherry Ballard, who has been with Blount since 1960, suggested I title this book "Good Morning, Cherry, How Are You Today?," explaining that over the years I have reported to the office more often by phone than I have showed up in person. I'm not sure whether she's kidding or not! Because she was our switchboard operator before we installed a direct-number phone system, Cherry is known within the company as "the voice of Blount.") Even in the 1950s, some people wondered how I could keep so many balls in the air at once — managing a business while simultaneously being involved in multiple outside activities. The answer was that I had good people working for me. I have always believed in giving people responsibility and giving them the right to fail. But they can't fail too many times. And if there's a problem, they have to let me know.

I also believe it's vital to develop management in depth by forcing senior people to groom their successors. Sometimes this is like pulling teeth. Once, John Caddell was heading off to Harvard Business School for a 13-week seminar. I said to Paul Hess that this would be a grand opportunity to see how the company ran without John and to designate someone to take his place for the 13 weeks. Paul, who was John's direct boss, responded that he could easily handle John's responsibilities himself and that, in any event, John would be only a phone call away. My friend Bob Bleke, who was present, swears that my face turned crimson and I almost had a heart attack. I barked, "I know you can run the place. I want to know who else can."

When the smoke had cleared, Paul designated Lloyd Williams to fill in for John. To make sure there was no backsliding, I instructed the switchboard not to place any calls to John at Harvard and admonished John himself that under no circumstances was he to phone the office for the next 13 weeks.

So in a sense, my being away from the office for extended periods reinforced my philosophy of giving others a chance to show what they could do. (And, unlike John at Harvard, I could always be reached by phone if the need arose.) Nonetheless, my frequent absences drove Paul Hess crazy. He thought I should spend more time in the business and less on all those other things I was doing. I disagreed. Being actively involved outside the company gave me perspective, and I made a lot of valuable contacts. It also embodied my belief that business people have a responsibility to help improve society. But we'll come to that in the next chapter.

THE BLOUNT PHILOSOPHY

WE want to create within the Blount organization a place where people can and will want to come and devote their lives toward building a more successful enterprise. To do so, we seek to create a climate where individuals can develop to their maximum potential. It is our belief that if people are set free to express themselves to the fullest, their accomplishments will be far beyond their dreams, and they will not only contribute to the growth of the company, but will also be more useful citizens and contribute to the larger society.

We hold a deep and abiding faith in the American enterprise system. We understand and have tolerance for a wide range of individual interpretations of this system, but we brook no adherence to any other way of life. We believe in a person's responsibility and duty as a citizen to look beyond the office, and we encourage participation in civic, cultural, religious, and political affairs in our country. We do not seek conformity; we do seek participation.

We believe we have no greater responsibility to the American enterprise system than to insure that our business operates at a reasonable profit. There is no way to provide opportunity for growth or job security other than to make profits. To accomplish this on a continuing basis, we believe it is necessary to grow. We believe growth is necessary to provide opportunities on an ever increasing scale for our people to make their mark. Therefore, we are dedicated to growth—growth as a company—growth as an organization—and growth as individuals.

This is what we stand for. This is what we are about.

A Tragic Accident

Amidst the good times, and there were many, we also encountered setbacks. In particular, we experienced a terrible tragedy at a job site in Tullahoma, Tennessee, where we were building the world's largest rocket test silo. The silo was shaped like an underground vacuum bottle. It consisted of a 250-foot-deep cylindrical hole; a nine-foot-thick concrete cap on top of the hole, with a round opening in the middle of the cap; a solid dome on top of the cap; and all sorts of complicated machinery and piping inside the silo. The huge facility was designed to test-fire rocket engines in a vacuum: an engine would be positioned under the dome, firing down into the hole. We had completed excavating the hole, and a subcontractor was pouring the first segment of the nine-foot-thick cement cap. I still remember the date: December 17, 1964. Just as the subcontractor finished one section of the cap, the framework beneath it gave way, dropping 800 tons of concrete into the hole, killing four workers. The accident occurred between shifts. Had it happened 30 minutes earlier or 30 minutes later, dozens of workers might have lost their lives.

I was in Montgomery and received a phone call minutes after the accident occurred. I flew immediately to Tullahoma, taking along my son Winton, then 20. On arrival, I visited each of the victim's families to express my personal devastation and assure them of Blount's support.

A federal board of inquiry was convened, ultimately ruling that the subcontractor had failed to put adequate supports under the cap. Because the supports, as installed, weren't strong enough, they had buckled under the weight of the concrete as it was being poured. The subcontractor was held fully liable. Even though our company was exonerated, the incident was a very sad one for all of us at Blount. Nothing could bring back those four men. Blount has never suffered another tragedy of that dimension, and I certainly hope we never will.

The Ups and Downs of Heavy Construction

I have already told you about our building division, headed by Paul Hess. We also had a heavy construction division, which built roads, bridges, dams and other infrastructure. Unlike the building division, the heavy construction division had its ups and downs. We finally closed it in the 1960s.

There was a time, early in our expansion program, when the heavy construction division nearly drove Blount into bankruptcy. This occurred in 1954 when we won a contract, in a joint venture with

Kansas City Bridge Company, to build a four-mile bridge across Mobile Bay to Dauphin Island. Unfortunately, the bridge spanned some of the roughest waters in the bay, and we had a dickens of a time putting it up. We lost $700,000 on the project, and we didn't have $700,000 to lose. I went to my friend Mills Lane, chief executive officer of Citizens & Southern Bank in Atlanta. Mills was the antithesis of the stuffed-shirt banker. He believed in people as much as he believed in numbers, and he was a flamboyant booster of civic causes. When the Braves baseball team was being romanced to come to Atlanta, he told the mayor, "You get the team, I'll find the money for the stadium," and showed up at the bank dressed in a baseball uniform to promote the idea. One of his favorite expressions was, "I'm going to rent you some money." So I visited Mills and told him about our losses on the Dauphin Island job. He asked, "What are you going to do?" I said, "Mills, there's only one thing I can do, go get more jobs and make it up." He said, "Go get 'em, tiger," and his bank loaned Blount the money to carry us through.

Our $700,000 loss in 1954 on this Dauphin Island bridge project in Mobile Bay nearly put Blount into bankruptcy. We had to dredge the bay to get the job done, and in doing so we accumulated a huge pile of shells. I came up with the idea of recouping some of our loss by selling the shells to pave roads on the island. Flying at the controls of a single-engine plane, with my friend Bobby Radcliff in the passenger seat, I told him of my plan. He became agitated and said I couldn't sell the shells because he owned the legal right to all the shells in the bay. I said they belonged to me because I had dredged them up. I finally put the plane into a nose-dive, and he shouted, "I give in, I give in." Once on the ground, however, he said he had acted under duress — that the shells still belonged to him. We eventually asked our lawyers to sort the matter out. However, by the time they went to Mobile Bay to view the shells, the pile was gone. Another contractor had taken them all, and neither Bobby nor I ended up with a penny.

Just as Mills Lane's bank was a key supporter of Blount, there have been others as well, including the Bradley Arant law firm, our outside counsel for the entire history of the company. We have been served by a series of exceptional lead attorneys at Bradley Arant, beginning with Mr. Bradley and Barney Monaghan in 1946. Barney became one of my best friends. In 1981, after my divorce, he wrote a letter I cherish, in which he expressed his desire to share in my future happiness. When I married Carolyn Varner, we invited him to our wedding. Carolyn and Barney had never met, although they knew about each other through me. As Carolyn and I entered the reception area following the ceremony, I pointed him out to her. She walked over to Barney and said, "Mr. Monaghan, I'm Carolyn Varner." He answered, "I'm so happy to meet you, and I want you to meet someone." He then introduced her to me — his way of teasing her that she had forgotten her name was now Blount! Barney and I had a special relationship that spanned many years, and his support and understanding meant a great deal to me.

When Barney left the firm in 1959 to become CEO of Vulcan Materials, Bradley Arant recruited a young Wall Street attorney and graduate of Yale Law School, Frank McFadden, to work principally with Blount. In 1969, Frank was appointed to a vacancy on the federal district court in Alabama and Tom Carruthers became our lead attorney. Tom went on to become the firm's managing director. Now retired as managing director but still with the firm, Tom continues as my personal attorney and close adviser. Our company's lead litigator today is Nick Gaede.

Sometimes things have a way of coming full circle. When Frank McFadden was first mentioned as a candidate for the federal bench in 1968, I told him, "If you want to change your pace, why don't you come work for us at Blount?" He turned me down, confiding that his heart was set on becoming a federal judge if selected. As fate would have it, the very next Saturday I received a call from President-elect Nixon, inviting me to join his cabinet. From my position within the Nixon administration, I was able to support Frank's candidacy — and with my support and that of others, he made it to the bench. Twelve years later, Frank came to see me and said he was leaving the judiciary for economic reasons. He had three young children and faced the expenses of their education, which could not be met on the low salaries then paid federal judges. Again, I invited him to join our company. This time he accepted, becoming the first general counsel in Blount's history. After a distinguished career — first as a partner in

Bradley Arant, then 10 years as a federal judge and the last 15 years as general counsel of Blount, coping with many complex problems in construction — Frank retired in 1995.

We launched the *Blount Banner* in the 1950s to communicate with employees across the United States. This issue from 1960 features our Univac computer. We were one of the first companies to use a Univac to aid in management control.

CHAMPIONING NEW IDEAS

Throughout the 1950s and 1960s, we led the construction industry in injecting some of the most up-to-date management techniques. I was constantly trying to be on the cutting edge, and I kept pushing our people to accept new ideas. If we wanted to be the best, I told them, we had to think and act like the best.

I observed, for instance, that many contracting companies were run by construction specialists. I believed we could gain a competitive edge by broadening the perspective of our managers. Therefore, beginning in the 1950s, we started sending our people to 13-week programs at Harvard, Virginia, Northwestern and other business schools.

Also in the 1950s, we were the first contractor to use the critical path method of scheduling and controlling a job. I believe this method was developed originally for the Manhattan Project to manage the complex process of inventing the atomic bomb. I read about this system in a magazine article, and it was clearly applicable to large construction projects. So we put it to work in our own business.

In 1960, we installed one of the first Univac computer systems to aid in management control.

Still further, I hired an industrial psychologist, Bob Bleke, to screen job candidates for management and management training positions. I knew about Bob from his work for Vulcan Materials and I took the idea of industrial psychology very seriously, even though some at Blount found the concept hard to swallow. I said to the skeptics, "When we interview prospective hires, we are not experts at looking inside them. We need a professional to do that for us and predict what kind of behavior we might expect." I also said, "Don't hire someone just because Bob Bleke says yes. But if he says no, don't touch that person with a 10-foot pole." We still use Bob's firm today.

Another innovation, beginning in 1956, was our annual meeting of key personnel, which gave Blount managers from across the country a chance to discuss common concerns and build morale. Initially, I brought in outside speakers from the financial and academic communities. However, our people found some of these speakers to be overly theoretical and dry. You could just see the heads nodding in the audience. Then one year I asked my friend Paul "Bear" Bryant, University of Alabama football coach, to speak at our meeting of key personnel. Now, that was a terrific decision. Bear was a great coach and a great manager. He started his speech by mumbling, "I don't know why Red asked me to give this talk. But let me tell you how we run our football program." He gave a wonderful speech on how to delegate authority and how to keep people accountable. His inspirational talk was a huge hit, and our managers couldn't wait to shake his hand and get his autograph. The lesson: sometimes you have to reach people's guts to reach their heads.

Throughout this period, I was trying to broaden my own business knowledge. In 1952, I joined the Young Presidents Organization, a national group of chief executives under 40 years old who were running businesses with at least $1 million of annual sales. In those days, a $1 million-a-year enterprise was a good-sized company. Later, I was elected YPO national treasurer. Through YPO, over a period of several years, I went to more than a dozen educational programs at Harvard and other business schools. Professors at these seminars kept driving home all kinds of business principles that we had already adopted at Blount by the seat of our pants. It was a real eye-opener, and it gave me enormous confidence that we were on the right path. Through YPO, I also met a great many other up-and-coming business executives from around the country, many of whom are still good friends. Part of my philosophy is to get out and make friends. The way I see it, you can never have too many people on your side.

WHY WE SOUGHT PRIVATE SECTOR WORK

In the mid-1960s, I got to thinking that almost all our work was for the federal government and maybe the time had come to diversify. One of the first big corporate construction jobs we went after was for a paper mill being planned by Union Camp Corporation in Alabama. After months of preliminary negotiations, the two Camp brothers, Jim and Hugh, who were married to sisters originally from Selma, Alabama, visited with us in Montgomery. It was clear that they were impressed by our one-of-a-kind projects for the government. They brought along their wives from Virginia, and I had them over to my home for lunch. Union Camp soon awarded us the contract to build its mill, even though we had no specific experience in building such projects. This job would prove to be the first of many paper mills we

would construct for various companies, and it opened the door to all kinds of other assignments from private industry. Moreover, after the Union Camp facility was completed, Hugh Camp invited me to become a director of Union Camp. I had to turn him down because I was joining the Nixon cabinet. He asked me again after I left government service, and this time I was happy to say yes, serving on the Union Camp board for the next 20 years.

We grew quickly in the industrial and commercial construction market. Indeed, by 1969, when I left for Washington, our business was split approximately 50-50 between public and private sector work. At that time, I made a dramatic decision: during my term as U.S. postmaster general, Blount would not bid on any government contracts. I wanted no possible appearance of conflict of interest. Overnight, I had slammed the door on half our company's market. The senior managers, in whose hands I was leaving the company while I was away, screamed bloody murder. But I stuck to my guns. I will return to this episode in Blount's history in a few pages.

Union Camp Corporation was one of our first major private-sector clients, beginning in the 1960s. We built the pulping operation, above, the paper mill, left, and other facilities for Union Camp, and this work gave us credentials to win more private-sector jobs.

CHAPTER FOUR

Politics and
Public Service

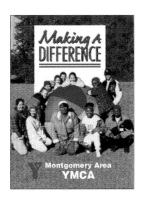

AMERICA HAS OFFERED ME ENORMOUS OPPOR-
tunity, and I want to give back as much as
possible. My dedication to public service is as
simple as that. Of course, many Americans
feel the way I do. Volunteerism and wide-
spread support of worthy causes — the idea
that people should help each other rather
than rely on the government to do it all for
them — helped make our nation great.

    As our company grew in the 1950s and
1960s, I became increasingly active in civic causes, from the local
YMCA to national political campaigns. My activities outside the
company exposed me to fresh ideas, brought me new friends and
helped fulfill my deep sense of obligation to the nation.

Opposite, I was privileged to serve in President Nixon's cabinet as post-master general. Here, we discuss postal reform. Left, the Montgomery YMCA is one of our city's most dynamic service organizations.

GETTING INVOLVED IN POLITICS

Some businesspeople steer clear of politics to avoid controversy
because they regard politics as a dirty profession. I think this attitude
is a mistake. Business is able to succeed because of popular support
for our nation's free enterprise system, and that support can evapo-
rate unless we play a constructive role in the political process and do
our part to help the community solve its problems. If we don't get
involved, who will? Do we want to leave politics entirely to the politicians? By definition, democracy thrives when as many citizens as
possible, from all walks of life, take part.

    Besides which, I relish a good political battle. It's great fun.

Growing up in Alabama, it was taken for granted that I would be a Democrat, and I was — at first. Alabama Republicans were such a tiny minority they were viewed as curiosities. There was only one Republican family in all of Union Springs in the 1920s and 1930s. They were considered so unusual that townspeople sometimes stared at them as they walked down the street. Political clout belonged entirely to the Democrats. For a candidate, winning the Democratic primary was tantamount to election. And for a voter, casting a ballot in the primary was the only way to have a voice in the selection of the local sheriff, mayor or any other elected official.

My first direct involvement in politics came in 1947 when, at age 26, I managed Joe Goode's Alabama gubernatorial campaign in Macon County. Goode, the state commissioner of agriculture and industry, had been a friend of my father. He was a conservative with a fine reputation, and just about everybody I knew thought highly of him. But then I had the rug pulled out from under me. Running a close third in the Democratic primary, Goode withdrew suddenly, throwing his support to the front-runner, "Big Jim" Folsom, one of the wily politicians in Alabama history. I was enraged and wrote a

I had tremendous admiration and respect for President Eisenhower, below. Opposite, my involvement in his 1952 presidential campaign got me on the cover of this magazine. In those days, supporting a Republican was quite radical in Alabama.

blistering letter to Goode, saying I had worked hard for him and he had sold out the conservatives and I couldn't believe he would do something like that. He wrote back in equally scalding language, suggesting something to the effect that I was an ill-mannered young ingrate. Folsom went on to win, in part because of Joe Goode's support. Goode sometimes ate lunch at the Elite Cafe in Montgomery. Not long after the election, I happened to see him there and went over to his table to explain why I had written the letter. All was quickly forgiven, and we subsequently got to know each other better and became friends. I don't know what I learned from this episode, except not to write nasty letters — although it did make me feel good to get my gripe off my chest.

My first involvement in national politics came in 1952, when I was drawn to the presidential candidacy of General Dwight Eisenhower. General Eisenhower was a leader who knew how to inspire people and command on the big stage. He not only led our nation and the western world in winning World War II, which for me and millions of other Americans was a defining time in our country, but was also the driving force behind the creation of America's interstate highway system, the largest construction project in history.

I met General Eisenhower two or three times during the 1952 campaign and found him to be cordial and quietly self-confident. He had the integrity, common sense and vision that our nation needed — and needs at all times. I was ready to go to the ends of the earth to help him become president.

WORKING FOR EISENHOWER

In fact, as late as 1951, the year before the election, nobody was sure whether Eisenhower would run. Both the Democrats and the Republicans were interested in having him head their ticket, but he did not make his intentions clear. In January 1952, for the first time, he revealed publicly that he was a lifelong Republican and said he would accept the Republican nomination if he received a "clear-cut call to political duty." Republican leaders then entered his name in various state presidential primaries, setting the Eisenhower bandwagon in motion.

Because Eisenhower was such a popular figure, there is a tendency today to think he was a shoo-in for the nomination once he made himself available. But that was not the case at all. Heading into the 1952 Republican convention, Eisenhower was locked in a tight race with Senator Robert Taft, the isolationist from Ohio. Taft actually had more committed delegates.

A few of us in Montgomery banded together to support Eisenhower's candidacy. The old-line Republicans in Alabama were all Taft people. However, when we tried to influence the Alabama party's choice, we found it difficult even to discover where the old-liners were meeting.

Republicans in the South were then referred to as "Post Office Republicans." Their major perk was to dole out patronage, especially local postmaster and rural letter carrier positions, whenever a Republican was in the White House. Unbelievable as it may seem today, these positions were political appointments subject to change whenever the presidency changed parties, and had been so for 200 years ever since Benjamin Franklin was postmaster general. Southern Republicans zealously defended their right to dispense this patronage and did not want any newcomers encroaching on their turf. In the South, this patronage was all the Republicans had, since there was virtually no chance that they would beat the Democrats in state and local elections.

One night, seven of us — all staunch Eisenhower supporters — gathered at the home of Dick Hudson, publisher of the *Montgomery Advertiser*, on Bankhead Avenue in Montgomery to plot our strategy. Certainly our organization was the first in Alabama for Eisenhower. I was elected the group's chairman. Years later, my son, Sam, bought that house, and today his former wife lives there with their children — my grandchildren. There is still a plaque over the fireplace, put there by Dick Hudson, commemorating our meeting. It reads:

> In this Room on the night of January 13, 1952 seven people with high hopes and purposes — Arthur Mead, Eugene Munger, W. M. Blount, Felix Shank, Grover Hall, R. F. Hudson, Jr., John Ashley — decided to pool their resources and their efforts to create a two-party system in Alabama through the nomination and election of Dwight David Eisenhower as President of the United States as a Republican. On November 4, 1952, the American people elected him President.

We were a bunch of young Turks who wanted to do our part to get Eisenhower elected. One of our tasks was simply to find out where the official Republicans were gathering. Many times they met in public phone booths, where two or three of them would get together, without publicizing the meeting in any way, to nominate the Republican candidates in private. Whenever we were successful in finding them, we would show up to promote Eisenhower. They certainly didn't appreciate our aggressive tactics. By the same token, we certainly didn't appreciate their unwillingness to open up the process to the views of others. Similar insurgencies were taking place all over the South on behalf of Eisenhower, infusing fresh blood into the Republican Party and marking the beginning of its rebirth in the South following years of dormancy.

Even though Alabama's entrenched Republicans ignored our pleas to consider General Eisenhower, I was not about to let them off the hook. Although I wasn't a delegate to the Republican national convention, I did obtain convention floor privileges and flew to Chicago in my single-engine Beechcraft Bonanza to lobby delegates from all the states on Eisenhower's behalf. I took along my sister, Barbara Lovelace, and a friend of hers. The head of the Alabama delegation, supporting Taft, was a prominent woman from Gadsden named Mrs. Noojin. Her husband was a Republican national committeeman. The 1952 Republican convention was one of the first political events to be broadcast nationally on live TV, and the cameras caught Mrs. Noojin and me right in the middle of an in-your-face shouting match on the convention floor. Viewers from coast to coast were able to eavesdrop as we got into a ferocious argument. She thought we were up-starts and said we were try-ing to invade their lair. And I told her we didn't want any patronage, we'd give them all the patronage, all we wanted was to get General Eisenhower nomi-nated and we were going to do everything possible to accomplish that.

To my delight, General Eisenhower captured the Republican nomination on the first ballot, even though Taft had entered the con-vention with a slight lead. There were contested slates of delegates from two states, Georgia and Louisiana. Judge Tuttle headed the Georgia delegation supporting Eisenhower, while the Louisiana del-egation supporting Eisenhower was headed by John Minor Wisdom, a distinguished lawyer from New Orleans. Both men made impas-sioned pleas to the convention that the Eisenhower delegates from their states should be seated, rather than the Taft delegates — and, in fact, the Eisenhower delegates did get seated, helping turn the tide in the general's favor. Following the election, President Eisenhower appointed Judge Tuttle and John Minor Wisdom to the 11th Circuit Court of Appeals.

I have been to many Republican conventions since then, but none has been as exciting for me as that first one in 1952.

Although I was not a dele-gate to the 1952 Republican National Convention in Chicago, I did obtain floor privileges and spent many hours lobbying delegates on behalf of Eisenhower. I have attended many Republican conventions in the intervening years, but none has, for me, matched the excitement of 1952.

Early in the 1952 election, Eisenhower's campaign staff created an organization called Citizens for Eisenhower to enable die-hard Democrats, including those in Alabama, to support the five-star general without calling themselves Republicans. I was appointed chairman of Citizens for Eisenhower for the state of Alabama and worked virtually fulltime on the campaign. Not long after my appointment, General Eisenhower called a meeting of all the Citizens for Eisenhower chairmen from across the country at the Brown Palace Hotel in Denver. General Eisenhower's wife, Mamie, was from Colorado, and the general himself liked to visit the state to fish with his father-in-law and friends. I flew to Denver in my Beechcraft Bonanza. Arriving at the hotel, I registered in the lobby, a seven-story-high atrium. When I got upstairs, the hotel staff had already put engraved stationary with my name on it in my room. That impressed this country boy from Union Springs.

Although Eisenhower ended up losing in Alabama to Adlai Stevenson by a whopping two-to-one margin, it was progress: in 1948, Dewey had lost the state to Truman by four-to-one! Moreover, Republicans made inroads all across the South. Eisenhower even beat Stevenson in Florida, Texas and Virginia, traditional Democratic strongholds. The long-standing Democratic domination of the South was beginning to weaken.

Looking back today, we Alabama Republicans have come a long way from those rag-tag days of 1952 when we were getting our act together. Beginning with the 1972 election, Alabama voters have now favored the Republican candidate in five of the past six presidential contests, a remarkable change in our state's political landscape. Today, the governor of Alabama is a Republican. One United States senator is a Republican, and I believe the other United States senator will be a Republican after the next election. The attorney general of Alabama is today a Republican, three of the seven members of the United States House of Representatives are Republicans, and I believe that will grow. Many of our mayors and other local officials are Republicans. Happily, the days of one-party politics, when the Democrats dominated our state, are gone. Winning the Democratic primary is no longer tantamount to election.

What has happened in Alabama reflects a significant change that has occurred all across the South. Today, many southern governors are Republicans, as are many senators, congressmen and local officials. The Republican Party has succeeded by appealing to the fundamental values that matter most to a majority of Americans.

It's a long way from 1952!

THE PRESIDENTIAL INAUGURATION

Inauguration Day was Tuesday, January 20, 1953. Under bright blue skies, Dwight David Eisenhower was sworn in as the 34th president of the United States and the first Republican to hold the office in 20 years. I had flown to Washington with a group of family and friends, including my buddy, John Overton, a rabid Democrat, to attend the ceremonies. Because of my role in having headed Citizens for Eisenhower in Alabama, I was able to obtain tickets for several events, including the inauguration itself. But John did me one better. Shortly after we arrived in Washington, John headed off on his own. In the next few hours, supremely self-confident as always, he managed to track down, introduce himself to and become friendly with influential members of the Eisenhower staff. Phoning me at the hotel, John announced, to my astonishment, that he was calling from the White House and had obtained tickets to several exclusive events on which I had struck out. That was vintage John Overton. When it came to getting tickets, he could be a Republican just like everybody else!

I would not have missed President Eisenhower's 1953 inauguration for all the money in the world. I returned home with many mementos, including this mock license plate.

Seventeen months following the inauguration, in June 1954, the following letter arrived in the mail:

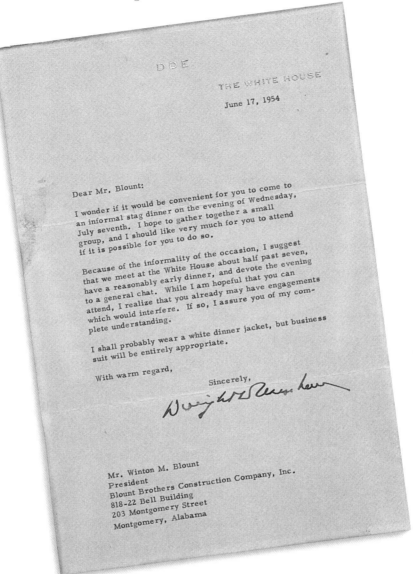

DDE

THE WHITE HOUSE

June 17, 1954

Dear Mr. Blount:

I wonder if it would be convenient for you to come to an informal stag dinner on the evening of Wednesday, July seventh. I hope to gather together a small group, and I should like very much for you to attend if it is possible for you to do so.

Because of the informality of the occasion, I suggest that we meet at the White House about half past seven, have a reasonably early dinner, and devote the evening to a general chat. While I am hopeful that you can attend, I realize that you already may have engagements which would interfere. If so, I assure you of my complete understanding.

I shall probably wear a white dinner jacket, but business suit will be entirely appropriate.

With warm regard,

Sincerely,

Dwight D Eisenhower

Mr. Winton M. Blount
President
Blount Brothers Construction Company, Inc.
818-22 Bell Building
203 Montgomery Street
Montgomery, Alabama

As it so happened, several months prior to receiving the letter, I had developed a terrible back problem. I couldn't even drive my car a block without having to pull over to the side of the road and get out to straighten up. I finally bought a Nash Rambler with a front passenger seat that folded down to make a bed, and I had someone drive me to the office each morning while I lay on the sleeper seat. In the office, I reclined on a couch as I worked. Eventually, when my condition didn't improve, I went to Memphis for a disk operation. In those days, a disk operation was followed by a lengthy recovery period. I was about one month into my recovery when I received the president's letter. Bad back or not, there was no way in the world I was going to say no to the president of the United States. On the appointed day, I headed for Washington in our company plane. Larry Harris, the first pilot I hired for the company, was flying, and I lay on a couch in the back of the plane. It was my first visit ever to the White House, that great symbol of American democracy. Dining in the White House with President Eisenhower and his invited guests was a thrill I shall never forget. While I have been in the White House many times since, nothing could compare to the first visit of a 33-year-old from Alabama.

REMEMBRANCES OF PRESIDENT RICHARD NIXON

I think President Richard Nixon has gotten one of the all-time bum raps in American history. I first met President Nixon in the 1952 presidential campaign, when he was Eisenhower's running mate. I was not active in the 1956 campaign, but in 1960, when Vice President Nixon ran for president, I got to know him quite well. For years, he was a popular whipping boy of the press, which loved to portray him as a nefarious schemer. That was not the Richard Nixon I knew. In my experience, he was gracious and forthright. And he was genuinely concerned about doing what was best for the country. I'll get to my views of Watergate, one of the most overrated "scandals" in American history, in the next chapter, when I will talk also about my relationship with President Nixon and the unqualified support he gave me when I went about the politically explosive task of reorganizing the U.S. postal system.

Richard Nixon lost the 1960 presidential election to John Kennedy by the narrowest of margins. Although some of his advisers wanted Nixon to challenge the results, he would not do so, believing that uncertainty about the election outcome would throw the nation into turmoil.

I became involved in the 1960 campaign because I knew Len Hall, Republican national chairman. When Vice President Nixon received the Republican Party's nomination, Len told Peter Flanigan, who co-chaired a volunteer group for Nixon-Lodge, to recruit me to run the campaign in the eight southeastern states. I accepted without hesitation and quickly established an organization in each of my assigned states. For the next several months, I traveled constantly in my plane up and down the eastern seaboard, from Virginia to Louisiana, making sure the campaign was running smoothly and drumming up support for the Nixon-Lodge ticket.

Vice President Nixon lost to John Kennedy in 1960. The race was exceptionally tight: Kennedy received 49.7 percent of the popular vote nationwide, Nixon 49.6 percent. In Illinois, Nixon lost by fewer than 9,000 votes out of nearly 5 million cast. There was a strong feeling within the Nixon organization that Illinois had been stolen by Chicago Mayor Richard Daley's Democratic machine through voter fraud. Voter fraud also seemed likely in Texas, where Nixon was defeated by 46,000 votes of nearly 2.5 million cast. (In his 1991 book, *One of Us: Richard Nixon and the American Dream*, liberal journalist Tom Wicker says charges of fraud in the 1960 election "were not merely the fulminations of poor losers." Wicker notes the "considerable possibility of vote fraud by Mayor Daley's redoubtable machine," and he adds, "The point is not that the election was stolen from Vice President Nixon but that it might have been, since it was so close. Republicans had ample reason to think it had been stolen.") A number of people in the Nixon organization felt we should challenge the election results. Vice President Nixon had gone to Key Biscayne, Florida, following the election — and he, too, believed there had been fraud. But when the idea of challenging the election outcome was raised by his advisers, he rejected it out of hand. He would not dispute the election, he said, because neither the country nor the world could stand the uncertainty of not knowing who was president. A court case challenging the results could have dragged on for months, maybe years, leaving the presidency in limbo and throwing the nation into turmoil. This is a side of Richard Nixon — his deep concern for the good of the nation — that I saw many times.

PETER FLANIGAN AND DON KENDALL

While Vice President Nixon's loss in 1960 was a great disappointment, it was through the campaign that I met Peter Flanigan, today one of my closest friends. Peter is now retired from Dillon Read, the investment banking firm. He lives in Westchester County, New York, and we often get together with our mutual pal, Don Kendall, the retired chief executive of PepsiCo, who lives across the state border in Connecticut. We hunt, ski or bicycle together, or just tell stories and have a grand time.

Don Kendall is today my closest friend. Whether it be politics, the arts, skiing, bicycling or socializing, we share many interests and enjoy a warm relationship. We also come from similar backgrounds. Don was born in Sequim, Washington, a community about the size of my hometown, Union Springs, Alabama. He didn't graduate from college; neither did I. He was a navy pilot in World War II, and, of course, I was an Army Air Corps pilot. He has assembled one of the country's great collections of sculpture. I, too, have been deeply involved in the visual and performing arts. Don's wife, Bim, is a beautiful, delightful and feisty German, and she and Carolyn have a great relationship.

Don is quite an individual. When he returned from World War II, he took a job driving a Pepsi truck, eventually rising to chairman and CEO, leading PepsiCo for more than two decades as it became one of the great corporations of the world. Because he spearheaded the globalization of Pepsi's business, he is one of the best-known and most admired executives not only in the United States, but also in Western Europe, Russia, China, India and elsewhere. It was he who arranged the famous Nixon-Khrushchev "kitchen debate" in 1959 at a trade fair in Moscow. In fact, Don was a great friend of President Nixon. Although Don did not hold a position in the Nixon administration, he headed many efforts supporting the president.

Don can be strong-minded and stubborn. We get into heated debates from time to time. Being with Don is never boring, and that's one reason we have such a good time.

MY TENURE AS PRESIDENT OF THE U. S. CHAMBER OF COMMERCE

Richard Nixon was elected president on his second attempt, in 1968, but this time around I was not part of the campaign. In May 1968, I was elected president of the U.S. Chamber of Commerce and was required by that organization's rules to be strictly "bipartisan." Being a Nixon enthusiast, I didn't know whether I could trust myself to keep my mouth shut or not. Just to be safe, during the Republican convention I rented William F. Buckley, Jr.'s schooner and sailed off the New England coast, out of reach of anyone who might ask my views. I took along my children and they loved it.

Incidentally, during my relatively brief tenure as president of the U.S. Chamber of Commerce, from May 1968 until President-elect Nixon asked me to join his cabinet later that year, one of my main goals was to find ways to control construction industry inflation, which had become rampant and was spilling over into the entire economy. I appointed Archie Davis, chairman of Wachovia Bank in North Carolina, who was on the U.S. Chamber board, to head our anti-inflation effort. We called our plan one that

I met President Johnson for the first time in 1968. As president of the U.S. Chamber of Commerce, I visited with him in the Oval Office to explain the chamber's anti-inflation program. Seated between us is Archie Davis, chairman of Wachovia Bank of North Carolina, who headed the chamber's anti-inflation effort. The president liked what he heard and endorsed our plan.

"the fellow pumping gas on the corner could understand." We visited President Johnson in the Oval Office and went over the plan, asking for his support, which he gave us. Our plan recognized that industrial companies were part of the problem and therefore had to be part of the solution.

Typically, if a company was building a new plant and the construction unions went on strike before it was completed, the company would tell the contractor, "Pay the unions what they want, just finish my plant." The company wanted to get its plant in operation as quickly as possible to start generating a return on investment — and it didn't care about the contractor's problems with the unions. The construction unions understood this and were using their leverage to negotiate hefty wage increases. To address these issues, the U.S. Chamber held a national seminar on inflation in the construction industry, bringing together general contractors, subcontractors, labor leaders and the CEOs of major companies. Steve Bechtel, head of his family's construction business, the largest in the nation, was there, as were many others. As chairman of the meeting, I was very outspoken about the power of the unions to bump up inflation. At one of the breaks, Steve said to me, "I don't know how you can be so tough with the unions without hurting your own business." I replied that I didn't believe I should alter my opinions just to suit my business needs. Shortly after this meeting, President-elect Nixon asked me to serve in his cabinet. Meanwhile, at the U.S. Chamber we had set up a "roundtable" of contractors, subcontractors, corporate CEOs and labor leaders to address common concerns, and I asked Steve to carry on this effort once I had left the U.S. Chamber. As part of this program, Steve enticed Roger Blough, the retired CEO of U.S. Steel who was highly respected in the business community, to head what we called Roger's Roundtable. This group was made up of representatives of leading industrial companies. We were quite successful in dampening construction industry inflation, and Roger's Roundtable evolved into the Business Roundtable, today one of the most influential business groups in America.

EDUCATION: A BEDROCK OF AMERICAN SOCIETY

Education is another of my lifelong passions. Currently, I am involved in a number of efforts, most notably Success by Six, aimed at helping youngsters in Montgomery be prepared by age six for success in school and in life. Success by Six illustrates my belief in the power of volunteerism and in forming coalitions that bring together diverse elements of the community to get things done.

In the fall of 1991, Police Chief John Wilson was the speaker at a Leadership Montgomery meeting. His subject was youth crime and drug use. He captured the attention of many of us when he said, simply and eloquently, that these were community problems, not just police problems, and the police could not handle them alone. The only effective way to nip them in the bud, he said, was for the whole community to get involved.

When John finished his remarks, I stood up and told the group that Carolyn and I had recently taken our granddaughter, Stuart Ann Varner, to her first-grade class in Birmingham. Stuart Ann's school is very innovative and creative, and it struck me that 50 to 60 percent of the other first-grade students in Alabama would never be able to compete with her and her classmates. Youngsters like Stuart Ann not only attend wonderful schools, but also come from loving and nurturing families. Often, they learn to count and read well before reaching first grade. By contrast, teachers have told me that many at-risk children enter the first grade not even knowing the sky is blue or the grass is green. It is vital to reach these at-risk children at the earliest possible age and to ensure that every child has proper nutrition, adequate medical care, positive preschool experiences and lots of love and attention from caring adults.

Success by Six was pioneered in Minneapolis. It combines various community resources, including health care and pre-school education, to foster early childhood development. I challenged Leadership Montgomery to work with me to bring Success by Six to our city, and the group readily accepted. There was instant support from a wide spectrum of the community.

We introduced Success by Six initially in one public housing community. The program is now in three additional neighborhoods, with plans to expand all over the county. I cannot think of anything in my life that has been more important than Success by Six, since it deals with the basic issue of helping young people succeed and assuring the future well-being of our society.

After that Leadership Montgomery meeting, I quickly recruited Bill Chandler, who heads the Montgomery YMCA, to co-chair Success by Six. With his leadership, Success by Six is now operating under the umbrella of the YMCA, with endorsement from the United Way.

Bill is one of the truly great people in Montgomery. We first met in the early 1950s and took an instant liking to each other, forming a lifelong friendship. Bill became the director of the Montgomery YMCA in the early 1950s, and it wasn't long before he

I cannot think of anything I am involved in today that is more important than Success by Six. Our objective is to ensure that every child born in Montgomery has the proper medical care, nurturing and pre-school education to be able to succeed on entering school at age six.

had me on the board of directors. I have been associated with the Y and played a principal role in every fundraiser we have had since, including the $4 million campaign going on as I write these words.

Bill is a dynamic, highly capable person and has dedicated his life to the YMCA and to Montgomery. Along the way, he also became head of Lion's International, travelling all over the world making friends and promoting that group's programs. I call on Bill whenever I become involved with major city problems — and he always accepts. How can you beat that? When Mayor Earl James appointed me chairman of the first biracial committee in Montgomery in the mid-1960s, I recruited Bill to be my co-chair. The committee was made up of an equal number of whites and blacks, and in those explosive times we helped bring the races together to find common ground and work out community problems. A great friend, Bob Nesbitt, a leader of the black community, was a key member of that group, offering wise counsel. Bob was also elected a director of the Montgomery YMCA when it became one of the first civic groups in Alabama to integrate its board, and he continues to serve on the YMCA board today.

UNIVERSITY OF ALABAMA

I have also been involved in higher education, serving on the boards of the University of Alabama and Rhodes College in Memphis.

In 1959, when I joined the University of Alabama board, I was 38 years old, a mere lad compared to my fellow trustees. The next youngest was nearly twice my age, something like 75, and several were in their 80s. Under the state constitution, terms were for life, and many trustees took that as an outright mandate never to retire. Furthermore, I was stunned to find that the board met only twice a year — at homecoming and commencement, when trustees were more inclined to take part in campus festivities than to sit in a board room pondering weighty issues. I got so upset that I told Dr. Frank Rose, the university president, I would resign unless the board became more than a figurehead group.

Change came slowly. But as younger and more progressive members were appointed to the board, and after much prodding, we all agreed to retire voluntarily at age 70. Later, we went to the state legislature and got them to enact a mandatory retirement age of 70 for University of Alabama trustees. In time, we also began to meet more frequently. Today, the university has a very active, talented board that plays a true oversight role.

As a University of Alabama trustee for 32 years, I was involved

I am a longtime member of the board of trustees of Rhodes College, a Presbyterian school in Memphis. I began contributing to Rhodes many years ago through my local church. However, in the 1960s, my church said Rhodes had become too liberal, and it cut off funding, so I began contributing directly. Subsequently, the college asked me to join its board, and I gladly accepted, serving for a number of years as chairman. Rhodes is a wonderful school. Our goal is to be the best liberal arts college in the United States. We are well on our way to getting there.

in many fascinating events, none more dramatic than George Wallace's decision to "stand in the schoolhouse door." Wallace had been elected governor in 1962 on a strict segregationist platform, vowing to defy federal orders to integrate Alabama schools. In June 1963, when two black students were about to enroll at the university, he said he would personally block their entrance by standing in the doorway to the registrar's office. That was his public declaration, intended to show he meant business, but behind the scenes he was quite nervous.

To counter Wallace's threat, President Kennedy federalized the Alabama National Guard, and 15,000 federal troops were stationed on campus as the expected confrontation approached. The day before the students were to arrive, the university board of trustees met all day in emergency session. Wallace was an ex officio member of the board, and though he seldom attended meetings, he did come to the emergency session to discuss his plans. The trustees were virtually unanimous in their view that the two students should be registered peacefully without interference by the governor. However, Wallace would not back down. I can still see him now. He kept talking in a monologue and was very much on edge (as we all were) because he didn't know what the federal government would do. As day gave way to night, the board kept meeting, trying to convince him to change his mind, but to no avail.

I happened to know President Kennedy's brother, Bobby Kennedy, the attorney general of the United States, having met him in the late 1950s when he came to Montgomery to speak to the Rotary Club; I had flown him back to Washington in my plane, and we had enjoyed a long, friendly conversation on that trip. Eventually, as the trustees' meeting extended into the evening, I suggested that I phone

This photograph of the University of Alabama board of trustees was taken shortly before I retired from the board in 1991. When I joined the board in 1959, it was made up of elderly white men. I was then 38 years old, a mere lad compared to my fellow trustees. We eventually got the state legislature to enact a mandatory retirement age of 70, and that marked the beginning of a transition toward today's younger and more diverse group.

Carolyn and I pose with President Ford. He and I are good friends and used to ski together in Colorado before he hurt his knee.

Below, this picture of then-Congressman George Bush and me has been called "the Great American Ballet." For some reason, the *Los Angeles Times* ran the photo on its front page when Bush was elected president.

Above, I posed with President Reagan and Vice President Bush at the time of their second inauguration in 1985. Left, I was a delegate to the 1988 Republican National Convention, which nominated George Bush for president and Dan Quayle for vice president. Carolyn and I had our picture taken with the candidates and their wives. Below, I visited with President Clinton and his wife, Hillary, when they invited the Business Council to the White House.

Bobby Kennedy at his home to see if we could work out a solution. The board agreed, and I went into Tuscaloosa to use a pay phone, since we suspected that all the phones on campus were bugged by the Feds. I called Bobby Kennedy at about 10 p.m. and explained that we were in the dark as to the federal government's plans. I also said we'd like to know how we might resolve this situation without disruption or violence. He said, "Stay right there. I'll call back in 15 minutes." He then phoned Nicholas Katzenbach, the deputy attorney general, who was on campus. Not long thereafter, Kennedy returned my call. He said the Justice Department was prepared to make a concession: it would allow Wallace to stand in the doorway and read his statement, if he would then step aside and allow the students to register. I went back to the board meeting with Kennedy's proposal. Wallace agreed, and there was a big sigh of relief. The scenario proposed by Bobby Kennedy went off without a hitch — and that is how the University of Alabama was integrated.

To be fair to Wallace, years later he renounced his segregationist views and was elected to a fourth term as governor in 1982 with a majority of the black vote — surely one of the most remarkable political turnabouts in American history.

CIVIL RIGHTS MOVEMENT

The 1950s and 1960s were a period of great civil rights turmoil throughout the South. TV images from that period show groups of angry whites assailing civil rights activists in the streets. That side of the civil rights period certainly existed and was reprehensible. However, there were also southern moderates, less visible, who worked for reconciliation and change. This side of the story is less well known.

I was convinced the South would solve its problems long before the rest of the country did, and I think it is turning out that way. Even though our schools were segregated, which was wrong, blacks and whites in the South knew each other and worked together and were able to communicate.

Treating people well, regardless of race, and obeying the law are values I learned from my parents. When Montgomery became engulfed in the civil rights crisis, I felt I had to stand up for the values in which I believe.

On a Saturday afternoon in May 1961, Freedom Riders arrived in Montgomery, having come down through Georgia and northern Alabama, seeking to end segregation in public facilities by traveling across the South in integrated groups. I was working in my office downtown when I heard reports, at about 4 p.m., that the Freedom Riders were being attacked at the bus station by a white mob. I was irate. At the time, I was president of the Alabama Chamber of Commerce. I immediately phoned Holman Head, a senior executive at our company and my executive assistant, and asked him to come to the office and help round up members of the chamber for an emergency meeting.

About 60 members showed up within an hour. The mayor of Montgomery, Earl James, and the police commissioner were there, as well. After a rather heated discussion, the members agreed to call on the police to protect the riders and end the violence. The vote, however, was not unanimous. One of those present was T. B. Hill, a promi-

Alabama Governor George Wallace "stands in the schoolhouse door." Publicly, the governor had vowed to prevent any black students from enrolling in the University of Alabama. Behind the scenes, however, the university trustees worked out a compromise with the federal government that allowed the governor to stand in the doorway, make a statement and then step aside to allow the students to enter.

nent older attorney who was active in the Democratic Party. I knew that T. B. had no great love for the Freedom Riders. But I also knew I needed his influence to win unanimity — and, besides that, he owed me a favor. In 1954, I had tried to get him appointed to the federal bench. Although he never did become a federal judge, he was grateful for my efforts. At the meeting, I turned to him and said, "T. B., why don't you draft this for us?" There was a brief look of surprise on his face, but he wrote the statement without protest. Perhaps because it came from his pen, everyone signed it, and we got the police to intervene and stop the attacks. The real hero of that day, however, was the head of the state highway patrol, Floyd Mann, who pulled out his pistol right in the middle of the melee and almost single-handedly drove back the white crowd. Floyd and I became close friends. We usually supported the same people politically and also civically. When Floyd died in January 1996, a large crowd of friends came to pay their last respects.

We learned an important lesson from the events of May 1961: preparation was essential to prevent violence in the future. As president of the Alabama Chamber of Commerce, I thought we had to get the business community involved. But it was like pulling teeth. At that time, Alabama business was dominated by major companies that had branches in the state. The heads of these operations were not really interested in Alabama. They had their eye on getting promoted to the home office in Pittsburgh, Detroit or wherever and did not want to hurt their chances by getting involved in anything "controversial."

Holman Head and I drew up a position paper entitled, "Where Alabama Stands," which stated a belief in treating all people with dignity and in compliance with the law. This kind of statement was revolutionary in the South at the time. I found it extremely difficult to win the approval of all the board members of the state Chamber of Commerce. But we finally did get their approval, and the chamber published the statement in newspapers and magazines all over the nation, such as the *Washington Post, U.S. News & World Report* and the *Wall Street Journal*, as well as in newspapers in Alabama.

The next big test came four years later, when the Selma-to-Montgomery march for voting rights, led by Martin Luther King, Jr., approached our city. Even though reports kept streaming in of violence along the route, Montgomery had made no preparations for the marchers' arrival. I went to Mayor James and asked that we hold a meeting of community leaders, including city and county officials, police representatives, businesspeople and a representative of the U.S. Department of Justice, to talk about how we were going to handle the march when it got to Montgomery. Many of those who agreed to attend did not want to do so downtown, because they feared the media would get wind of our gathering. (It was not popular in those days to be publicly associated with anything that seemed to support the civil rights movement.) We therefore met in my home, which is about five miles east of downtown Montgomery, in what was then still rural countryside. As the meeting neared its conclusion, we had resolved most of the major issues, including the march route into the city and police protection. Suddenly, there was a knock on the door. The room immediately turned silent, with people glancing at each other wondering whether some enterprising reporter had latched on to our get-together. But it turned out to be Ramsey Clark, a Justice Department official who later became attorney general in the Johnson administration. He had heard about our gathering from other Justice Department officials and wanted to be part of the discussion. He had come directly from the march, muddy boots and all. He was not very helpful.

There was no major violence within the city limits when the marchers arrived from Selma, and out of that effort, Mayor James appointed the first biracial committee in Montgomery and asked me to serve as chairman. This was the committee on which Bill Chandler and Bob Nesbitt also served. Over the next few years, our committee sought to build bridges between the black and white communities and foster compliance with civil rights laws.

At the same time, at the Alabama Chamber of Commerce we organized business seminars across the state to meet the federal equal access laws. For instance, we held seminars for restaurant owners so they would realize they weren't alone in integrating their facilities (a common fear among retail businesses was to be the first in a community to integrate and then find that competitors weren't doing the same) and would understand from these meetings that the state Chamber of Commerce supported compliance.

We had our share of problems in Montgomery. We were far from perfect. There was defiance, yes. And there was violence. But there was also the ability to surmount the violence and move ahead.

During this turbulent period, nobody ever stopped me on the street to complain about what I was doing. However, businesspeople did occasionally take me aside to ask why I was taking such "controversial" stands. They'd say, "It's going to hurt your business." I didn't believe that then and I never did. And even if I had, I don't think you can water down your personal beliefs to suit your business needs. If you run your life that way, you'll never stand up for anything.

"THAT'S NOT MY BAG !!"

CHAPTER FIVE

Postmaster General: Feeding Them Grits Till They Said Yes

I HAVE BEEN CALLED THE FATHER OF POSTAL reform, "the man who took the Post Office out of politics," in the words of one magazine. This unexpected turn of events in my life began on a Saturday afternoon in November 1968, shortly after the presidential election. I was having a great time at the Alabama-Auburn football game. The stadium was filled to capacity and the crowd was yelling its lungs out when I was approached by an emissary of President-elect Nixon. Somehow he had found me in the stands, and he bore a message: the president-elect wanted to talk with me by phone. Immediately after the game, I went to a friend's house to return the call. Although I had not had any contact with Nixon during the 1968 campaign because I was president of the U.S. Chamber of Commerce and had to be nonpartisan, there was speculation in the press following his victory that he would ask me to be his secretary of commerce or some other position. I followed these reports with interest, but was in the dark like everybody else.

When I returned Nixon's call, he was not available. However, I did speak with one of his aides, who delivered some surprising news: the president-elect wanted me to be in his cabinet as postmaster general, an office I had never imagined, even in my wildest dreams, that I would one day hold. A friend who was in the room heard me reply, "The Post Office! How did they come up with that idea?"

In our conversation, the aide said the president-elect wanted to reform the Post Office and needed a tough-minded businessman to do it.

Opposite, editorial cartoonists had a grand time commenting on the battle for postal reform.

The Post Office, the nation's largest civilian employer, plays a unique role. No other institution touches the life of virtually every American each day with a needed service. Its smooth functioning is essential to our economic well-being.

For 200 years, however, the Post Office had been managed not to maximize performance, but to maximize patronage. The Post Office was the greatest single source of political pork in federal government. Members of the House of Representatives of the party which held the White House nominated all 40,000 local postmasters and all 35,000 rural letter carriers across the nation. These jobs were handed out to party loyalists. Moreover, promotions within the postal service were based on political connections, not merit. Congress also determined postal employee salaries, decided how much should be spent on research and development, established the price of a first-class stamp and even decreed where new post office buildings should be constructed.

Although Congress maintained a stranglehold on postal operations, it conceded one major task to the postmaster general: dole out the patronage. Befitting his position as a skilled political operative, the postmaster general had the most magnificent office in Washington. It was built in the 1930s when Jim Farley, the legendary Democratic deal-maker, was postmaster general. As the story goes, Farley asked who had the largest office in Washington — and was told it was that of Harold Ickes, secretary of the interior. Farley directed that the new Post Office Department building be constructed so that his would be even larger.

Indeed, the postmaster general's office was well over half the size of a basketball court, with a marble fireplace at each end. And next to it was an ornate oval reception room, with a row of chairs along its wall in which people seeking favors from the government would sit each morning. Jim Farley would walk around that reception room, accompanied by an aide with a pad, and talk to each person and ask what they wanted. He did not invent this system. Handing out patronage was what the postmaster general had always done, dating back to the times of Ben Franklin, who founded the U.S. postal service in the eighteenth century.

Because of this absurd system of mismanagement and twisted priorities, the Post Office had fallen hopelessly behind the times. Postal clerks were still sorting mail into cases with 49 partitions (the same pigeon-hole box designed by Ben Franklin in the 1790s), after which it was placed in sacks, lifted onto trucks and handled an average of 10 additional times before reaching its destination. Given these inefficiencies, it should not be surprising that Americans paid twice for their mail service — in postage and in tax subsidies. By 1968, one-quarter of the $9 billion needed each year to operate the Post Office came from federal tax appropriations.

These problems came to a head in 1966, when operations broke down at the Chicago post office, the world's largest. Postal clerks in Chicago could not keep pace with their workload, and boxcars of undelivered mail had to be shunted onto sidings for days at a time, all the way to New York to the East and the Rocky Mountains to the West. Recognizing the urgent need for change, President Johnson appointed a blue-ribbon committee, headed by retired AT&T Chairman Frederick Kappel, to study the postal system and recommend ways to modernize its operations. The report of the President's Commission on Postal Organization, or the Kappel Commission, as it was familiarly known, was issued in June 1968, proposing major actions to de-politicize the Post Office and improve its performance. Once issued, however, the report just sat there gathering dust, as do most Washington committee reports. Nobody in the government seemed to want postal reform after all, especially Marvin Watson, the postmaster general before me. The political gravy that flowed from the postal trough was simply too great, and members of Congress were unwilling to give up control.

The postmaster general had the largest and most magnificent office among all the members of the president's cabinet. It was built in the 1930s at the direction of James Farley, FDR's postmaster general. In this picture, showing one end of the office, I am sixth from the right. President Nixon is directly to my right. Ted Klassen, my deputy postmaster general, is directly to my left. At far right in the picture is Paul Carlin, my point man with Congress, who later became postmaster general.

Although I had not heard of the Kappel Commission report when I talked with the president-elect's representative on that Saturday afternoon, somebody told me about it after our conversation and I obtained a copy and read it before going to New York to meet with Mr. Nixon the following week. I took along my son, Sam, who was wearing his Marine Corps uniform. The president-elect, a family man and a strong supporter of the military, gave Sam a warm welcome and invited him to sit in on our meeting.

In our conversation, the president-elect said he was looking for a postmaster general who would take the Post Office Department out of politics and restructure its operations to make them efficient and effective. I told him I had read the Kappel Commission report and thought it offered a blueprint for change. I also said, "Mr. President, if you want to reform the Post Office, I'd be delighted to do it. If you want a postmaster general like the rest of them, I'm not interested." He assured me he wanted reform, which he had pledged in his campaign. And when I asked, "Who's going to make the appointments in the Post Office?," he pointed that long bony finger at me and said, "You are." In other words, the White House would not interfere. In the months and years that followed, President Nixon never wavered in that commitment, and his total support in the face of intense political opposition made postal reform possible.

GETTING STARTED

When I told my brother, Houston, I was taking a leave of absence from my company to become postmaster general, he thought I was crazy — literally. But he agreed to help. I put all my investment and business holdings into a blind trust, and Houston took over as chairman of Blount Brothers Construction Company while continuing to work full time at Vulcan. He soon hired Austin Paddock, administrative vice president of U.S. Steel, to run Blount as president and chief executive officer while I was away. I did not return to the company for four years.

My confirmation hearings went smoothly. I began my testimony before the Senate committee by saying, "Gentlemen, I want you to know that William Blount, who signed the Constitution and was the first governor of Tennessee and the first United States senator from that state, was one of my ancestors. I also want you to know he was the first United States senator ever to be impeached. And you heard it from me. You can look it up." My ancestor, William Blount, a

I was sworn in as
postmaster general
by Chief Justice
Earl Warren
on January 22, 1969.

Founding Father, was forced to resign from the Senate in 1797 when he plotted to help Britain wrest Florida and Louisiana from Spain. Impeachment is like an indictment; it is not a conviction. He proudly got on his horse the next day and went back to Tennessee, where he later was elected governor. His half-brother was governor of Tennessee from 1815 through the early 1820s and sent Andrew Jackson to Alabama to fight the Battle of Horseshoe Bend, the last battle of the War of 1812.

By the time my confirmation hearings were over, I had just about finished recruiting an exceptional team of nearly 50 business executives. I felt that to run an organization as large as the Post Office, with 750,000 employees, we really had to get down into the depths of it, and doing so required a lot of help. I knew many of these people, or their bosses, from my term as president of the U.S. Chamber of Commerce, and I simply went to them and made my case. High-ranking businesspeople left their jobs to join the Post Office because they believed our nation needed a strong postal system free of politics. I still appreciate very deeply their unselfish assistance.

No other postmaster general had ever managed the Post Office as our team did.

- I recruited E. T. "Ted" Klassen, president and chief operating officer of American Can Company, to be deputy postmaster general. Ted was a specialist in labor relations and was very helpful when we faced a national postal strike (more on that later). He was deeply involved in day-to-day operations of the Post Office, enabling me to devote major efforts to postal reform.
- Frank Nunlist, former CEO of Studebaker, was in charge of postal operations.
- Jim Josendale joined our operations team from Wirerope Corporation, where he was CEO.
- Hal Faught, former division general manager of Westinghouse, headed our research and development program.
- David Nelson, a partner in Squire, Sanders & Dempsey, became our general counsel. After postal reform, I asked Dave to join Blount's board of directors. He did so, later resigning to become a federal appellate judge.
- Jim Hargrove, senior vice president of Eastern Gas Transmission, was recommended to me by Peter Flanigan. Jim became our assistant postmaster general for finance and administration. He later served as U.S. ambassador to Australia in the Ford administration and, after that, was a director of Blount.
- Paul Carlin came to us from the National Audiovisual Association and the National School Board's Association in Washington. He was my point man with Congress. Paul stayed with the Postal Service and later became the 66th postmaster general. That, in itself, was unprecedented. Before reform, there was no opportunity for people to rise within the ranks of the Post Office based on merit. Most postal jobs were dead-ends, which was devastating to morale.
- Bill Dunlap came to us from Procter & Gamble, where he was a marketing manager. He developed a detailed plan for marketing postal reform — identifying objectives, establishing strategies, targeting audiences, etc.
- Jim Henderson, who died in 1995, was a very talented advertising executive from Greenville, South Carolina. He was my special assistant for public information.
- Jim Holland, Henderson's successor, conceived many innovative ideas for communicating our reform message to the public.
- Tom Ellington, another advertising executive, came to us from Young & Rubicam.
- Ron Lee, a former White House Fellow who had helped spear-

head the idea of forming the Kappel Commission, was another key player in our efforts to win passage of reform legislation.

• Ken Housman, director of human resources at Union Carbide, became our assistant postmaster general for employee relations.

• Bill Sullivan, a staff member of the Kappel Commission, worked with Ron Lee in the planning area. He later was a governor of the United States Postal Service and has been vice chancellor of the University of Maine for the past 15 years

• When I asked my friend Dick Helms, director of the CIA, for the best person to head the Postal Inspection Service, he recommended Bill Cotter, CIA associate director. Bill later was a vice president of Bunge Corporation, the grain exporter. He died in 1995.

• Noel Koch, who later served as assistant secretary of defense, helped me write speeches. He now has his own consulting business and continues to assist me in that area today.

I wish I had the space to name all the others.

With our team in place, we systematically went about the process of building public support for reform. One of my priorities, even before taking office, was to enlist as many influential allies as possible from both parties, starting at the very top. I knew President Johnson through my leadership of the U.S. Chamber of Commerce. Visiting him in the closing days of his administration, I asked if he would support the Kappel Commission report in his farewell State of the Union address. Marvin Watson, President Johnson's postmaster general, was very much opposed to the Kappel recommendations, and he was just going up in smoke about my attempts to influence the president. President Johnson and I talked, but I didn't learn of his decision until I heard the speech: he endorsed the report.

President-elect Nixon asked each of his cabinet members to make a courtesy call on President Johnson in the White House before the Nixon administration took office. Although President Johnson had chosen not to run for reelection in 1968, he was still an astute politician, ever the campaigner. The first thing he said to me was, "I would have beaten the crap out of Nixon if I had run." We had a good time at our meeting and he seemed to enjoy my visit. Later, he was an important ally in postal reform.

President Nixon was inaugurated on Monday, January 20, 1969. Fifteen days later, I went to the White House press room and announced that we would no longer appoint any local postmasters or rural carriers by the congressional system. Within minutes, the belly-aching could be heard all the way from Capitol Hill. Republicans, who had been squeezed out of postal patronage for the past eight years when Democrats were in the White House, were furious. There were currently more than 2,100 postmaster positions vacant, and Republican congressmen were just salivating at the prospect of filling those jobs. They could not believe they were being denied their turn. Bryce Harlow, the administration's director of congressional relations, warned President Nixon he would be "committing hara-kari" if he supported what I was doing. In an interview years later, Harlow quoted Republican Congressman H. R. Gross of Iowa as having said of President Nixon, "That son of a bitch takes away all the job opportunities Republicans have been crying for for a generation."

In late February, the President invited Bryce Harlow and me to breakfast at the White House to discuss our conflicting views. Bryce complained that I had ignited a congressional "firestorm." He proposed a solution: continue the patronage system for at least a year to give Republicans a chance to even the score a little, and after that he might be able to support reform. I responded, "Mr. President, I've thought about this a lot. Bryce is right that people are angry. But we're dealing with a Congress that is two-thirds Democratic. If we continue the current system for a year, which sounds reasonable, it will prove we are not sincere. You don't get a little bit pregnant. You either do it or not." I also said, "Somebody has to pay the price, and if we want postal reform, it is the Republicans who have to walk the plank." Without hesitation, the president agreed. He promised to continue to back my efforts no matter how many times I had to take the case for reform up to the Hill. But he also cautioned that, in his opinion, reform legislation could not be passed until Congress was controlled by the Republicans. I appreciated his support, even if I didn't concur with his prognosis.

President Nixon stuck with me, just as he promised. In April 1969, in his State of the Union address, he said postal reform was one of the goals of his administration. Six weeks later, in May 1969, we sent Congress our proposed legislation, drafted by David Nelson, my senior assistant postmaster general and general counsel, based on the Kappel Commission report. There was great skepticism that the legislation would even make it out of committee. But I don't take no for an answer easily. I have a relentless quality that seems to inspire some people and drive others nuts. I also happen to love a challenge.

HOW WE GOT IT DONE

The next 15 months would be one of the most intense periods of my life. I have never worked harder, and I gained a lot of respect for those in government who devote incredibly long hours to their jobs.

We formed a bipartisan group, the Citizens Committee for Postal Reform, and I flew to Texas on a government plane to see President Lyndon Johnson again, this time asking his help in rallying Democrats to join this group. He drove me around his ranch as we talked, ultimately pledging his support. After lunch, he took me to the little airport on the ranch, and I got in the plane to depart. President Johnson left, and we were taxiing out to the runway, when the control tower called and asked that we come back. I didn't know the reason, but we taxied in and I got out of the plane. It turned out that Mrs. Johnson wanted to say good-bye. "I'm sorry I didn't get to

see you after lunch," she said, and she gave me a gift of homemade preserves to take back to Washington. Her thoughtfulness was, as always, greatly appreciated. She's a very gracious lady — really something else, a delightful person.

It was through the assistance of President Johnson that Larry O'Brien, a former postmaster general and a prominent Democrat, agreed

to co-chair the Citizens Committee for Postal Reform together with former Republican Senator Thruston Morton of Kentucky. O'Brien had been the Democratic national chairman, Morton the Republican national chairman, so I had heavy hitters from both parties on our side. In newspaper ads, the Citizens Committee listed three major goals of reform:

- Reorganize the Post Office Department on a self-supporting basis as a nonprofit government corporation;
- Modernize outdated facilities to ensure dependable and efficient service; and
- Improve working conditions and career opportunities for postal employees with true collective bargaining between labor and management.

The Post Office Department building was located at the corner of Pennsylvania Avenue and 12th Street, five blocks from the White House. I visited the president a number of times as we worked for postal reform. He made a return visit in August 1970, 18 months into my term, to sign the Postal Reorganization Act, a bill he had earlier predicted would pass only when Republicans controlled both houses of Congress.

In addition to the national committee, we formed local groups in cities across the United States. I went on the road to give speeches and meet with newspaper editorial boards, drumming up grassroots support. Many newspapers favored reform. It was such an obviously good idea. Nonetheless, many doubted it would actually happen. The *Roanoke World News* editorialized that passing the reorganization bill would require "one of the minor political miracles of the century."

When not on the road, I promoted postal reform at every opportunity in Washington — in testimony before Congress, at social gatherings, at press conferences. My strategy was to meet with nearly every member of Congress at least once. This was done in groups of one to six members, where I explained the objectives of postal reform and responded to each of their concerns.

In March 1969, when I sensed that the political pressures within the Republican Party against reform were not abating, I asked Gerald Ford, the Republican House minority leader, for the rare opportunity to meet with all Republican House members at a closed-door session. He granted my request, and for two-and-a-half hours I did my best to pluck the thorns of anger many of them were feeling from their loss of postal patronage. Still, they kept up the heat, so I returned 10 days later for a one-and-a-half-hour session. In both cases, I responded directly and forthrightly to the congressmen's individual concerns. The tone of the meetings was tempestuous. Even as I write this, I can still recall the many barbed comments as if these events occurred only yesterday.

The president had a yacht, the *Sequoia*, which was rarely used by other members of his cabinet. I used it all the time, taking senators and congressmen up and down the Potomac to wine and dine them and argue my case. My breakfasts became a Washington ritual. I invited groups of senators and congressmen and fed them southern grits and quail every morning. One of the invitees was heard to say, "If we don't pass postal reform and get Blount out of town, he's going to kill us with those grits."

Congress isn't used to dealing with someone who never gives up. When they knock someone down, he usually goes away. I didn't.

The postal unions were fierce in their opposition to reform. The unions liked the status quo because it gave them clout with Congress. Any time the unions wanted Congress to grant a raise or enact other legislation, their members would descend on Capitol Hill, filling the corridors, and Congress would eventually cave in. Members of Congress liked the system, also, because it was a source of patronage. On top of that, whenever a congressman ran for reelection he could count on the postal employees in his district, who were beholden to him for their jobs, to help with his campaign.

Iowa Congressman H. R. Gross, the ranking Republican on the House Committee on Post Office and Civil Service, was a persistent critic of reform. He was a cantankerous fellow who couldn't say enough bad things about our proposed legislation. The battle for postal reform centered in the House Post Office Committee. Within the committee, one of our greatest allies was Congressman Edward J. Derwinski, the second-ranking Republican member. Ultimately, I enlisted Morris Udall, the well-regarded congressman from Arizona, on the Democratic side.

A Republican congressman, Bill Scott of Virginia, was a particular pain in the neck. A steady stream of leaks was emanating from the Post Office Department; many department employees had close ties to Congress and were feeding confidential information and half-truths to the House committee to undermine reform. We established a rule that members of the Congress could not talk to the employees of our government relations department without going through our public relations department. I did this to ensure that the Post Office spoke to Congress with a unified voice. But even more important was my conviction that I did not want anyone in the Post Office cozying up to any member of Congress, sharing confidential information. I was determined that the Post Office be run like a private corporation

I took the case for postal reform to the public through frequent media appearances and speeches. This appearance on *Meet the Press* occurred in June 1969, shortly after the Nixon administration had introduced reform legislation in the Congress. To my right is moderator Edwin Newman.

by the professional management team I had assembled. Shortly after I issued this rule, Congressman Scott said to me during a public hearing, "Mr. Blount, if you stick to this plan, it will make you the dumbest man in Washington." Being fed up with Congressman Scott anyway, I snapped back, "Mr. Congressman, it takes one to know one." This exchange went into the *Congressional Record*, and old-timers in the Post Office Department were shocked. Scott later was named by the press as the "dumbest man in the Congress." He took the floor of the House to debate the charge, thereby proving how dumb he was.

The situation in the Senate Post Office and Civil Service Committee was not nearly as difficult as it was in the House. Senator Gale McGee of Wyoming, though a Democrat, supported what I was trying to do. As chairman of the Senate committee, he was particularly helpful in derailing postal union efforts to obtain an outsize wage increase; he stuck firmly to the idea that any increase should be tied to the passage of postal reform legislation. When the president of Iceland died, President Nixon asked me to head the United States delegation to the funeral. I took along, as members of my group, Senator McGee and his wife, as well as the Republican senator from Colorado.

I got to be good friends with Senator McGee, as well as with Ted Stevens of Alaska, a Republican on the Senate committee. In fact, Senator Stevens asked me to go to Alaska to help with his first reelection campaign. He is still in the Senate today and says he would not have won that first time he was up for reelection if I hadn't gone with him. While there, Senator Stevens took me on a moose hunt organized with Alaskan flair. We traveled in a big vehicle built to go over the tundra, while helicopters flew overhead trying to locate a moose. The people of Alaska are very friendly and I loved them all. But my heart was not into the high-tech hunt. I finally shot a moose. When they wanted me to gut it, I said, "No way, I don't want the moose." So they gutted it for me and shipped 300 pounds of moose meat to my home in Washington. Every evening when I came home, I could smell that moose meat cooking — hamburgers, steaks, whatever. I started giving it away, but ran out of enemies.

President Nixon sent me on one other mission to represent him

Postal reform was a bipartisan issue, drawing support from both sides of the aisle, although tentatively so at first. Key early backers included Edward Derwinski, the Republican from Illinois, left, and Morris Udall, the Democrat from Arizona, right.

when the president of Bolivia was assassinated. My party included Charles Meyer, the assistant secretary of state for Latin America; a lieutenant general; a protocol officer from the State Department and one other person. We traveled on Air Force II. Shortly after we were airborne, I asked one of the attendants about plans for our return flight. He said Air Force II would fly back immediately to Washington and they would send another plane to pick us up. That shocked me because, as a pilot, I knew how much it would cost to send a huge plane empty from Bolivia to Washington and another huge plane empty from Washington to Bolivia. I told the pilot this was ridiculous and I wanted him to get on the radio and tell them to change his orders, that he was to wait in Bolivia for the return trip. He said he could not do that because the Air Force wanted to fly down an empty plane for crew training. I insisted that he call and get his orders changed. By the time we were over Panama, he came back to the passenger compartment and said they had agreed to the change in plans and Air Force II would wait on the ground until we were ready to go. That episode shows how mindless bureaucracy can sometimes be. It also demonstrates that you can defeat bureaucracy if you are persistent enough.

The trip was memorable, to say the least. It wasn't at all clear who would succeed the slain Bolivian president. When we arrived at the airport, situated at an altitude of 12,000 feet, the streets were filled with troops, and several rival factions were threatening civil war. I presented my credentials to the acting president in his office, amidst the ominous sound of soldiers running up and down the building's stairs, which were in the open air in a large atrium. During the funeral procession two days later, the streets were lined on both sides with groups holding up signs and yelling at each other. The motorcycle police accompanying our motorcade kept turning into the crowd to drive the people back. The tension was incredible. We left Bolivia still uncertain as to who would be the new president. The matter was later settled peacefully.

BACK IN WASHINGTON

I returned to the United States with the fracas over postal reform still going hot and heavy. Because the postal unions opposed reform and I was looking for all the help I could get, I phoned George Meany, head of the AFL-CIO, and asked if he would see me. He agreed to a meeting at his office. Although Meany had been a member of the Kappel Commission, he had objected to some of its recommendations and therefore did not sign its report. Nonetheless, he under-

MODERN DAY PAUL REVERE

stood the issues thoroughly. We were having lunch one day, and Mr. Meany said, "You know, you're the first president of the U.S. Chamber of Commerce who has ever been in my office" — even though the AFL-CIO and the U.S. Chamber are located within a block of each other. That comment seemed to cement our relationship. I talked with him about postal reform, and we arrived at a basic agreement as to the labor provisions of the legislation. Meany obviously could not undermine the postal unions, which belonged to the AFL-CIO, but he did try to be a voice of reason with them. He was straightforward and helpful. Lane Kirkland, who succeeded Meany as head of the AFL-CIO, later remarked that by the time postal reform was enacted only two people had kept their word, George Meany and Red Blount.

As the battle for postal reform became more heated, I became the subject of newspaper editorial cartoons, ranging in tone from derisive to skeptical to admiring. I still have a collection of them hanging in a stairway at my home. One of the more amusing, published during my initial days as postmaster general, was by Herblock in the *Washington Post.* It shows a post office building with mail piled helter-skelter on the roof and bulging out the windows, with the caption, "Under new attempt at management."

One of my least favorite persons in Washington during this time was the columnist Drew Pearson. Although he kept phoning me to discuss postal reform, I wouldn't talk with him because I thought he'd do a hatchet-job. Rightly or wrongly, Pearson got mad and found an opportunity to strike back. As postmaster general, three Filipino waiters were assigned to me by the government. One morning, arriving at my office at 7 a.m., I found them sitting at my desk opening my mail. I fired them on the spot and got Jesse Butcher, a marvelous fellow who had worked for me as a chauffeur in Alabama, to come to Washington. Jesse single-handedly replaced all three and did the job with efficiency and grace. However, Drew Pearson got wind of the firings and wrote an article about me and my arrogance and my Versailles-like office and how I had hired this crony from Alabama to serve as my assistant. In fact, my "assistant" was my cook, and he deserved every penny he earned. I've got thick skin, but I worried that Jesse, not used to the rough-and-tumble of politics, might be upset about having been raked over the coals in the press. The day Pearson's article appeared, I arrived at the office about 7 a.m. Right away, Jesse said, "Mr. Blount, did you read the paper this morning?" I replied, "Sure did, Jesse." He asked if I thought Pearson's arti-

Opposite, as this cartoon suggests, the need for change was urgent. Postal clerks were still sorting mail into the same type of pigeon-hole box designed by Ben Franklin in the 1790s. Pictured below is Jesse Butcher, my cook. Look at that smile. Isn't it beautiful?

cle was in the Alabama papers. And I said I thought it was. A big smile spread across his face. He was thrilled to be a celebrity. He carried that article with him till the day he died. At the slightest provocation, he would take it out of his wallet and show it to his friends at the Elks Club in Alabama.

In March 1970, the stakes were escalated when the postal unions went on strike. Although there had been numerous strikes against the postal services of Canada and England, this was the first strike in history against any agency of the United States government. Strikes against the federal government are illegal in our country, and the unions' action threatened a constitutional crisis.

The threat of a strike had been brewing for some time. The unions had wanted Congress to give them a raise and asked for my support, but I didn't think they deserved a raise. I made clear that, in any event, I was not inclined to endorse their request until postal reform, which they still opposed, was enacted. Upset at my attitude, the unions went directly to the Congress, whereupon some of my allies in the Senate blocked legislation granting them a pay hike.

Soon thereafter, a postal strike erupted in New York and spread across the country to many other cities. If the unions could play hardball, I could too. So I went to the president and asked that he call out the National Guard to move the mail. Despite vocal opposition from Secretary of Labor George Shultz, who feared there would be nationwide sympathy strikes by other unions, the president went along with my request, mobilizing the New York National Guard. As the strike spread across the country, a high-level White House delegation came to see me. It included Secretary of Labor Shultz (a perennial favorite of President Nixon), the head of the Federal Mediation and Conciliation Service, Bill Usery (who himself later became labor secretary), presidential aides Bob Haldeman and John Ehrlichman, congressional liaison Bryce Harlow and White House press secretary Ron Ziegler. They sat in a semi-circle around my desk. As they began to talk, it became clear they wanted to take control of negotiations with the postal unions. I told them, "Gentlemen, you can get a new postmaster general, but as long as I am postmaster general, you are not going to take control of this strike." They seemed shocked. After a few moments, George Shultz got up and started toward the door, saying he knew when he wasn't wanted. As he got to the door, I replied, "George, don't go away mad." The others left shortly thereafter, and that was the last I heard about their taking control of negotiations with the unions.

A sympathy strike never did occur, and two days after the National Guard was called out, the postal employees returned to

work. I had told the unions I wouldn't even discuss wages so long as their members were on strike. After they had returned, we held around-the-clock negotiations and reached an agreement early one morning at about three a.m. The settlement amounted to billions of dollars. According to U.S. law at that time, if one federal department granted a raise it applied to all the other departments, to the members of Congress and even to the military. I did not have the authority to make an agreement of such magnitude. Therefore, seven hours after having completed negotiations with the unions, I met with President Nixon in the Oval Office. It struck me that I was presenting him with a monumental problem. After I told him of the quandary I had created, he related his own experience of having gone to Pittsburgh as vice president to help settle a national steel strike in 1959. That experience, he said, taught him that you have to give responsibility to the man on the site — and he supported my agreement with the postal unions.

The agreement with the unions granted something to both sides. The unions got their raise... but not right away. I got something because the wage increase was appended to the postal reform bill in the Congress.

The 1970 postal strike, the first ever against the United States government, was settled with the signing of a labor agreement in the offices of George Meany, president of the AFL-CIO. Mr. Meany is third from right at the table. I am fourth from right. In my dealings with Mr. Meany, he always kept his word and was very helpful in making postal reform possible.

Slowly but surely, the tide shifted toward reform. Articles such as a *Life* magazine cover story, "The U.S. Mail Mess," helped keep the topic in the news, making it increasingly difficult for senators and congressmen to explain to their constituents why they opposed reform. Moreover, members of the Congress did not want to be held responsible for another postal strike, which might have occurred if they failed to pass reform legislation, which contained the promised wage increase. There was never a moment when I said, "Eureka, we've made it." However, by early summer 1970, I could see it was going to happen — and it did. On August 6, 1970, the Postal Reorganization Act was passed with bipartisan support. The final vote was an overwhelming 339-29 in the House, 57-7 in the Senate. Six days later, President Nixon traveled the five blocks from the White House to the Post Office Department to sign the bill into law. Among those present were six of my predecessors, including Jim Farley and Larry O'Brien. In his remarks, the President said, "We have accomplished something that very few thought could be accomplished even 18 months ago." The *New York Times* called the legislation the 91st Congress's "first historic achievement," one that "promises to give American mail service the first morale boost it has had since the pony express." On the other hand, Congressman Gross complained that the bill had "taken the post office away from the American people," and, more pertinently, "the Congress." Some people never know when to sing a new tune.

The legislation replaced the Post Office Department with the United States Postal Service, an independent establishment within the federal government, free of congressional interference. The only major compromise we had made to get the legislation passed was to withdraw our plan that postal rates be set by the postmaster general. We felt the ability to establish prices was part and parcel of the ability to manage the Postal Service, as is true in any private-sector company. However, Congress just wasn't ready to allow that, and we ended up agreeing to the creation of a separate Postal Rate Commission. This arrangement is awkward. However, Dave Nelson drafted the legislation to include an escape clause that gives the Postal Service some degree of price control. The postmaster general recommends rate changes to the Postal Rate Commission. The commission then holds hearings and accepts or modifies the postmaster general's proposal, sending its decision back to the board of gover-

Soon after taking office as postmaster general, I was interviewed by *U.S. News & World Report.* In the interview, I noted that the Post Office Department was plagued by archaic equipment, outdated management methods and inadequate capital investment. One of my goals, I said, was to "bring this department — kicking and screaming — into the last third of the twentieth century."

nors of the Postal Service, which can override the Postal Rate Commission by unanimous vote.

Under the legislation, the Post Office Department was given up to one year to transform itself into the United States Postal Service.

Changing the Post Office

Former AT&T Chairman Fred Kappel, the man who helped start postal reform, once said of his company, "The Bell System is like a damn big dragon. You kick it in the tail, and two years later, it feels it in its head." The same could be said of the Post Office, an equally complex and massive organization.

We faced many challenges as we prepared to convert the Post Office Department to the Postal Service. These included a multitude of issues ranging from revamping our organizational structure, to setting up districts across the country and staffing them with competent managers, to training our people, to establishing new banking and borrowing relationships, to redesigning our logo and printing new stationery and signs. The historic changeover took place on June 30, 1971, less than a year after the Postal Reorganization Act had been signed into law.

Has reform paid off? You bet it has. One of the best-kept secrets in America today is the success of the United States Postal Service. Although people love to gripe about the mail, in fact, the Postal Service is the biggest and most cost-efficient postal system in the world. When I was postmaster general, we delivered 80 billion pieces of mail a year and had 750,000 employees. Today, the United States Postal Service delivers 190 billion pieces of mail a year (40 percent of the world's total) with the same number of employees, one of the greatest productivity increases in the country. Furthermore, it charges the lowest first-class postage rates of any industrialized nation. And all of its income now comes from the sale of stamps, not a penny from taxes, making it an exceptional arm of the U.S. government — one of the few that is financially self-supporting.

But reform was only part of the story. During my tenure as postmaster general, our management team worked very hard to bring the Post Office into the twentieth century.

• Shortly after reform was enacted, we engaged the Harvard Business School to establish special programs to train our managers. The Post Office had never provided its people with such training before.

• We developed programs to recruit and promote employees based on merit, not politics.

ANOTHER CONSTRUCTION JOB BY RED BLOUNT

This is one of the editorial cartoons that hangs in the stairway of my home. It captures my sense of pride and accomplishment in having guided the Post Office Department through an historic period of restructuring and modernization.

• We invested in modern equipment to begin to automate the processing of mail, thereby reducing costs and speeding service.

• We set delivery standards for the first time as a benchmark to measure our performance.

• We introduced new services, such as express mail and mail-gram.

• We eliminated air mail as a premium-cost service. All first-class mail is now transported by air, at no extra charge to the customer, where doing so provides the most rapid delivery.

• We arranged with the State Department for local post offices to accept passport applications, part of our effort to make the Postal Service more consumer-friendly.

In addition, several of our people, led by Wib Walling, were deeply concerned about the problems of the inner cities. We saw a synergy between these problems and our requirements: people in the inner cities needed jobs, the Postal Service needed qualified temporary employees. As a result, in one of our most innovative programs, we established storefront academies in cities around the country, providing training to people who had dropped out of high school. In doing so, we gave these individuals temporary employment while they studied for their high school degrees. On graduation, some went to college, others stayed with the Postal Service in full-time positions.

It was a wonderful program. But you can't imagine the grief it caused. Our teachers were selected from the inner cities. We sent them to New Mexico for special training, similar to Outward Bound, to imbue them with self-confidence. Some newspapers in New Mexico wanted to be know why the state was being invaded by "outsiders." And Congress launched hearings into the theory of the storefront academies — why we were doing this and how much it cost. Ultimately, we were vindicated: in 1972, the Office of Management and Budget evaluated the storefront academies and found them to be "one of the most successful programs in the country in dealing with hard-core dropouts."

Someone said recently that it seemed out of character for a Republican like myself to care about unemployed people in the inner city. But you might be surprised. Republicans have compassionate instincts, too.

ATTACKING THE DRUG LABS

I am a high-energy person who is always looking for new challenges. After postal reform had been enacted, I was casting about for new themes for speeches and I asked Noel Koch, one of my aides, for suggestions. He came up with the idea, for a speech in Dallas, that I urge Americans to boycott French goods unless the drug labs in Marseilles, then a major source of illegal drugs in the U.S., were closed. I thought the idea was great, and the speech was a real stemwinder. My comments made front-page headlines throughout France, whereupon the French government angrily filed a protest with the State Department. Scrambling for cover, the White House issued a statement saying my views did not represent official policy of the U.S. government. For my next speech, I turned up the heat and said the same thing all over again. Some people felt I was overstepping my bounds. Nonetheless, the speeches had the desired result: the drug labs were put out of business by the French. But the French ambassador never did invite me to another party at the embassy.

MY ATTEMPT TO DELIVER MAIL TO THE POWs

I had a number of other unusual experiences while serving as postmaster general, none more memorable than my attempt to visit Hanoi during the Vietnam War. I was completely supportive of the war, even though some of my children were adamantly opposed. My son, Tom, came to Washington to participate in antiwar demonstrations, as did many young men and women of his generation. We put Tom and some of his friends up at our home when they were in Washington for the protests. I respect and love my children even when I do not agree with what they have to say.

For Christmas 1970, I went to South Vietnam to make sure the mail was being delivered to the troops in the field. En route, we made a refueling stop at Guam, where the B-52s which bombed Vietnam were based. I met the commanding officer, Lieutenant General Al Gillem. He took me out to the runway in his jeep, and we sat there watching the B-52s thunder off into the night toward enemy territory. I had flown the B-29 Superfortress in World War II, but the B-52s were massive in comparison. When I got to South Vietnam, one of the first things I did was get permission to fly out to "Charlie country" in a helicopter to watch the B-52s drop their bombs. Very dramatic!

General Gillem now lives in Montgomery with his lovely wife, Beth, and we remain good friends.

In South Vietnam, the generals tried to button me up in Saigon

In 1969, on a trip to Vietnam to make sure the mail was getting through to the troops, I visited Hill 55 west of Danang. Nearly 30 years later, in 1996, while taking part in ceremonies to open a Blount training and distribution center in North Carolina, I was approached by a representative of the North Carolina Chamber of Commerce who said he had been a soldier on Hill 55 at the time of my visit. He said a bunch of GI's were sitting in a tent when they heard the postmaster general was coming to see them at their jungle outpost. One of them blurted out, "What the hell's wrong with him? Is he crazy?"

and just give me briefings. I said, "No, I want to talk with the troops." I ultimately did that, visiting installations up and down the nation. First, we flew west to a mountainous region that is home to the Montagnards, diminutive Vietnamese who are fierce soldiers. I talked with GIs and saw wounded soldiers being airlifted by helicopter to base hospitals. Then we flew northeast to the huge airbase at Danang. From there, I flew by helicopter to four or five bases in the field and even fired a cannon into enemy territory.

But it occurred to me that the biggest challenge faced by the Post Office in Vietnam was whether the mail was getting through to American soldiers being held prisoner in the north. Therefore, after returning home, I made plans to go to Paris to meet with members of the North Vietnamese delegation to the Paris peace talks in hopes of getting permission to visit the north and talk with the POWs. My friend Henry Kissinger took a very dim view of my plan and tried to discourage me. However, I insisted, and the State Department finally helped. Thus began an unusual odyssey across Europe and North Africa.

In Paris, I met a couple of times with the North Vietnamese delegation, but it was obviously not productive. So I went to Bucharest to seek the help of the Romanians, who were close to the North Vietnamese. I knew the president of Romania, Nicolae Ceausescu, having sat next to him at a state dinner in the White House. He met with me, but nothing came of that either. From Bucharest, I went to Budapest to talk with the Hungarian government — and promptly got involved in the negotiations to free Cardinal Jozsef Mindszenty.

For those too young to remember, the Roman Catholic cardinal was a rabid anti-communist who was accused by the Hungarian government of treason and illegal monetary transactions. At a sensational public trial in the late 1940s, he pleaded guilty to most charges, although it was widely assumed he had been drugged to obtain a confession. Convicted and imprisoned, Cardinal Mindszenty was freed by rebel forces in the 1956 Hungarian revolution. When the revolution was crushed, he took refuge in the U.S. embassy and stayed there, becoming a worldwide symbol of opposition to communist tyranny.

I happened to arrive in Budapest when the U.S. ambassador, who represented the interests of the Vatican in that country, was negotiating with the Hungarian government for the cardinal's release. By that time, Cardinal Mindszenty had been cooped up in the embassy for 15 years, and when I talked with him he was as crazy as a bedbug. Who wouldn't have been? There had been nothing for him to do all those years except walk back and forth in his room or outside in a small area. He was now nearly 80 years old. In our conversations, he kept talking about communists. He thought they were in the embassy, outside the embassy, everyplace you might imagine. He was just obsessed with the topic.

By the early 1970s, the Hungarian government wanted Cardinal Mindszenty out of the country, but the conditions under which he could depart were in dispute. When I arrived at the embassy, the American ambassador was about to attend a meeting at the Hungarian foreign ministry to talk about the terms of the cardinal's release, and he invited me along. The negotiations centered on two main issues: whether the Hungarian government or the Vatican would name the next cardinal, and whether Cardinal Mindszenty would leave the country by plane, as the government wanted, or by car, as the Vatican wanted. Because I was the highest-ranking government official to visit Hungary during the Nixon administration, I was allowed to participate in the talks and played a minor role in their resolution. Under the deal reached that day, the Vatican got to name his successor and the cardinal left by car, but he agreed to do nothing to stir up the Hungarian people as he traveled through the countryside. Cardinal Mindszenty left Hungary shortly thereafter.

Despite the success of the negotiations to free Cardinal Mindszenty, Budapest was fruitless in my quest to enter North Vietnam. As in Paris and Bucharest, I was offered promises but no concrete help. So I went to Algeria, another country friendly with North Vietnam. I met in Algiers with the foreign minister, and after that I traveled to Geneva to seek the assistance of the International Red Cross.

All of them agreed to help, but they didn't do a damn thing. Despite my efforts, I never did get into North Vietnam to see the POWs. It was a worthwhile effort. It just didn't work out — a great disappointment.

Above, Apollo 11 astronauts Michael Collins, Neil Armstrong and Buzz Aldrin join me for the unveiling of a mock-up of the "First Man on the Moon" stamp. The astronauts had taken a postage-stamp die to the moon and back, and the stamps were printed from that die — a unique way for the Post Office to celebrate their historic mission. Right, when President-elect Nixon announced that I would be his postmaster general, the *Alabama Journal* took pride in noting that a native son would be joining the Nixon cabinet.

Right, President Nixon invited Mamie Eisenhower to the Oval Office to present her with a first-day issue of the postage stamp honoring her late husband. Mrs. Nixon and President Nixon look on as I discuss the stamp with Mrs. Eisenhower. It was a very moving occasion for me.

Above and right, President Nixon backed me every step of the way in making postal reform possible. Even though he took tremendous political heat for doing so, he never wavered in his support.

RED BLOUNT
Candidate for United States Senate
He can do it

PD. POL. ADV. YOUTH FOR BLOUNT, DEVERE McLENNAN, BIRMINGHAM

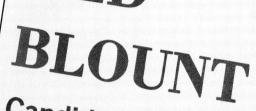

Red Blount
He can do it!

RUNNING FOR THE U.S. SENATE

At the end of 1971, having completed the assignment the president had given me — to shepherd postal reform through the Congress and reorganize the Post Office Department — I submitted my resignation. I had served as postmaster general for three years and was ready to move on.

Rather than returning immediately to my company, I had decided to run for the United States Senate. John Sparkman, the Democratic incumbent, was up for reelection in 1972. I had always thought about running for governor of Alabama. But there was no governor's race in 1972. So I took a shot at the Senate. I got swamped.

Two years earlier, in his 1970 gubernatorial campaign, George Wallace had used me as a punching bag. Virtually ignoring the candidate he was running against, Wallace acted as if he were competing against me, even though I was living and working in Washington, devoting my energies to postal reform. One of the editorial cartoons hanging on the staircase wall at my home shows a young boy saying to his father, "Daddy, if Wallace is running against the postmaster general, the mean old judges and the big newspapers, who's running against Brewer?" Wallace would bring a bedsheet up to the dais and peek under it, saying, "Who do I see under there? I see the postmaster general." He called me a rich war contractor up in Washington telling Alabamans how to vote. And he claimed my house in Montgomery had 26 bathrooms and lavish stables. (Our house has six bathrooms. While that may seem like a lot to some people, it's a big house — and six is a far cry from 26.) That was vintage George Wallace. I didn't know whether to be flattered that I was so important to him or angry that he was besmirching my name.

When I ran for the Senate in 1972, many of these same charges were recycled by Sparkman. The airwaves were filled with campaign ads about my "26 bathrooms." But I really got sandbagged when President Nixon, while sending his brother to campaign for me, gave indirect support to Sparkman. At a crucial moment in the contest, the president dispatched his plane to Alabama to pick up Sparkman in a very publicized way, saying Sparkman was needed for a vote in the Senate. (He was not needed.) And the president indicated on another occasion that Sparkman's continued presence in the Senate was important to the administration. President Nixon was himself running for reelection that year, and Republican campaign materials in Alabama featured the Nixon-Blount team. Although his comments hurt my campaign, I completely understood what President Nixon was doing. The Senate was still going to be controlled by the

Opposite, in 1972, when I ran for the United States Senate, I enjoyed the campaign and met a lot of wonderful people. Unfortunately, I was trounced by John Sparkman, the longtime Democratic incumbent. I am not one to linger on setbacks. I put them out of mind and move on to the next challenge.

Democrats, and the President needed to stay on good terms with the senior Democratic members of that body. I never took umbrage and I never talked with Nixon about the matter.

I was less than thrilled, however, with the many bankers from around the country who sent a flood of money to the Sparkman campaign but gave barely a penny to me, a businessman who had been president of the U.S. Chamber of Commerce. The bankers had a jaundiced view. Sparkman was chairman of the Senate Banking Committee — and the bankers were petrified that if he lost the election, the committee chairmanship would fall to the next ranking Democratic member, William Proxmire, the pesky senator from Wisconsin. The bankers loved Sparkman. They hated Proxmire, a maverick if ever there was one. The bankers got their wish: Sparkman beat me decisively, retaining his Senate seat. However, they ended up losing the war. Not long thereafter, despite the dedication of the bankers to his reelection, Sparkman quit the Banking Committee to join the Senate Foreign Relations Committee as chairman, and was succeeded as chairman of the Banking Committee by the dreaded Proxmire. I still joke with my friend Mark Hatfield, the former Republican Senator from Oregon, who helped with my 1972 campaign, that this was indeed poetic justice.

The 1972 Senate campaign was the only time I ever ran for public office. I realized I would have been miserable in the U.S. Senate. As governor you are a manager and can get things done. But in the Senate you are just one of 100 dukedoms. You have to compromise to get things done, and that's not my cup of tea.

WATERGATE

Although I was no longer in Washington when the Watergate break-in and its aftermath occurred, those of us who had been part of the Nixon administration had our concerns about the uselessness of a presidency being torn down by something that was not very important. Watergate should have been a tiny footnote, if even that, on the pages of American history. In every presidential race prior to 1972, and every one since, both sides have tried to find out what the other side is doing. That does not make the Watergate break-in right; it was a violation of the law. But it was small-time stuff compared with the political hijinks in many other presidential elections.

The problem was the way the disclosure of Watergate was handled. If John Mitchell, Nixon's campaign chairman, had said right at the beginning, "Yes, I ordered this done, I take full responsibility and I am resigning," Watergate would have faded quickly from the headlines. In my opinion, President Nixon — who did not know about the attempted burglary until after it had occurred — would never have been toppled. Unfortunately, President Nixon allowed himself to believe that the truth about Watergate — that it involved members of his staff — might destroy his chances for reelection in 1972. So he ordered a cover-up, and that was his downfall. The terrible irony is that President Nixon did not need to suppress the facts. His margin of victory in the election turned out to be so great that the Democratic candidate, George McGovern, could not possibly have won even if the truth about Watergate had been known.

Instead of looking at that one incident, the entire presidency of Richard Nixon offers a completely different picture of the administration and the man. I think, and many observers agree, that he was our smartest president in the twentieth century and perhaps extending back further. He understood the forces shaping the world and knew how to respond to global events. When it came to Nixon's great foreign policy achievements, such as the opening of China to the West, it is sometimes said that Kissinger was the teacher. But he was not. Nixon was the teacher, Kissinger the student. In addition to postal reform, during his presidency he launched the war on cancer and brought about the peaceful desegregation of schools in the South. All Americans owe him a great debt of gratitude for protecting our air, waters and land by establishing the Environmental Protection Agency. He also initiated the policy of detente with the Soviet Union, ended the United States military involvement in Vietnam and worked toward a lasting peace in the Middle East.

You can't ignore Watergate. It happened. What should not be obscured, however, are Nixon's historic accomplishments to make the world a better place. I am proud to have served in his cabinet.

President Nixon's accomplishments were legion and included the opening of China to the West, detente with the Soviet Union, the ending of American military involvement in Vietnam, the establishment of the Environmental Protection Agency, postal reform and many others. I believe history will recognize Richard Nixon as one of the great presidents of the twentieth century.

CHAPTER SIX

Back to Business:
Diversification on
My Mind

I RETURNED TO MY COMPANY AT THE BEGINNING of 1973, initially as chairman of the executive committee while Austin Paddock continued as president and CEO. A lot had transpired in the four years I was away, including:
• A string of acquisitions, some of which made sense, most not;
• Blount's transition to becoming a publicly owned company, a move I fully endorsed; and
• Blount's survival and growth despite my having lopped off half its markets.
I had a lot of catching up to do.

Opposite, we were in the specialty steel business from 1979 to 1988 through our ownership of Washington Steel Corporation. Left, one of our earliest diversification moves was into agribusiness, including the manufacture of grain bins and tanks.

SUCCEEDING UNDER FIRE

As you may recall, Blount grew in the 1950s by specializing in federal fixed-price construction projects. In the 1960s, we increased our emphasis on building commercial and industrial facilities for corporations. By 1968, we had roughly a 50-50 split between government and private-sector work.

On being named postmaster general, I had directed that Blount could no longer bid on any federal projects so long as I was in government service. Blount was a private company and I owned all the stock at that time. When I told President Nixon of my decision, he said, "You don't have to do that. You just can't allow them to do business with the Post Office." "Mr. President," I said, "I'm interested in my own reputation as well as yours. I'm not going to let the newspapers write that Red Blount had a drink with Mel Laird [Nixon's secretary of defense] and three months later his company got a $50 million job with the Defense Department." The only way I knew to avoid all perception of conflict was by barring my company from any federal assignments.

As I discussed in Chapter 4, my decision to do so drove Blount's managers up the walls. But I left for Washington so quickly they didn't have much time to protest before I was out the door. In any event,

I had great confidence in their abilities. And I also believed that giving up all government work to concentrate on private-sector jobs was an opportunity as much as a challenge, since it would change Blount's focus toward the private construction market, which was growing. ("An OPPORTUNITY? That's a bunch of hogwash," John Caddell exclaimed not long ago when being interviewed for this book. John headed our construction division in the 1970s and early 1980s. "Half the business was wiped off the books. It made us work like hell!") True enough. But John and his colleagues rose to the challenge. They got busy finding more private-sector work, and I think it made us a stronger company in the long run. So that part of the company's performance was impressive, and I give John and his people all the credit in the world.

John Caddell joined Blount in 1952 as a $75-a-week estimator fresh out of Georgia Tech. With his intelligence, tenacity and penchant for hard work, he advanced rapidly in the company, becoming president of our building division in the early 1970s, succeeding his mentor, Paul Hess. John stayed with Blount until the 1980s and later bought our construction business when we divested it.

Less impressive was the diversification that took place while I was away. Let me step back a minute before explaining why this diversification was so ill-conceived.

From the earliest days of the company, I thought Blount would one day diversify and become more than a contractor. Construction was just the business we happened to start in, and I believed that by developing a well-rounded team of management generalists — as opposed to construction specialists — we would be able to succeed in any business we wanted.

In 1960, I began monitoring several other construction companies which were public companies to see how they were performing relative to Blount. I also thought we might learn something by studying their business strategies and management techniques. One firm, Utah Construction & Mining Co., immediately caught my eye. Utah was a well-established enterprise, nearly 100 years old, which had built many large projects in the West, including Hoover Dam in partnership with the Bechtel Company. It was publicly owned, with a majority of the stock held by three Mormon families. In 1960, Utah earned $1 million, which was not much for a company of its size. That same year, however, Ed Littlefield, from one of the three families, became Utah's chairman and chief executive officer. I watched with fascination as he fueled Utah's earnings growth by shifting the company's business from heavy construction, which was less profitable, into mining and transportation worldwide, which were more profitable. By the mid-1970s, the company, renamed Utah International, Inc., was earning nearly $100 million a year. Now that really got my attention! He then sold Utah to General Electric for two-and-a-half billion dollars. I came to know Ed Littlefield in the 1960s and 1970s and we still run into each other occasionally, primarily at meetings of the Business Council, to which we both belong.

Utah Construction's highly successful diversification strategy became a model for what I wanted to accomplish. I set out to change Blount. From the late 1960s to the early 1990s, Blount entered a series of businesses as we recast our corporate profile. We had been entirely in construction during our first 20 years of existence. Today, half a century after our founding, we no longer have any construction and are entirely in manufacturing. This fundamental change in direction has been enormously profitable for Blount and its shareholders. As you will see, we used the profits from construction to invest in other businesses. We then used the profits from some of these businesses, as well as from our huge Saudi Arabian construction project, to buy Omark Industries, which today forms Blount's nucleus.

HEADING DOWN THE ACQUISITION TRAIL

We began diversifying in 1967, the year before I left for Washington, when we acquired the Benjamin F. Shaw Company of Wilmington, Delaware. Shaw fabricated and installed piping systems for power and chemicals plants. With a staff of 3,500 mechanics, it was one of the largest mechanical contractors in the United States.

The history of Shaw would make an interesting book in its own right. The company was started in 1893, at a time when manufacturing plants were just beginning to switch to electrical power from steam and water. Shaw grew with the power generation industry. By World War I, it was deemed so important to the national economy that its entire facilities and most of its personnel were loaned to the Du Pont Engineering Company, construction agent for the United

In 1947, my childhood friend Sam Wilson was working at a bank in Union Springs when I convinced him to join Blount as one of our first employees, beginning as our office manager. He stayed with Blount nearly four decades, retiring in 1984 as vice president in charge of business development. It was Sam who first heard that B.F. Shaw Company was available for acquisition.

States government; Shaw played a significant role in building World War I-related manufacturing plants as rapidly and inexpensively as possible.

In the 1960s, however, third-generation management ran this once-prestigious company into the ground. When I heard about Shaw from Sam Wilson, who headed our business development team, it was in the third year of a five-year Chapter 11 reorganization. I believe Sam had learned of Shaw from a Blount client.*

I was on the lookout for acquisitions, and Shaw seemed to fit my criteria for an initial deal to get our feet wet: a construction-related business available at a reasonable price. The company had three major customers, the largest being Du Pont. Before agreeing to the acquisition, I went personally to all three and asked if they would like us to get involved. I was not interested in buying Shaw if any of these three customers planned to sever its relationship. They all agreed to stay, and I negotiated with the creditors' committee to acquire the company. It wasn't a difficult deal to consummate; the price was only a few hundred thousand dollars. Through this transaction, I began to learn the process of acquiring a company, including the critical importance of looking for the problems.

We revitalized Shaw, and it became a very profitable business for us. The company had plants in Wilmington, Delaware, and Tuscaloosa, Alabama. Two years after the acquisition, we built a large facility in Laurens, South Carolina, for the fabrication of nuclear and

fossil power plant piping. By 1978, a decade after the acquisition, Shaw attained record revenues of $120 million, nearly one-quarter of Blount's total that year. My son, Winton, was chairman of Shaw for several years and led it through much of this growth. Subsequently, we merged its operations into Blount, whereupon Shaw lost its separate identity. Although we no longer tracked its revenues or profits, by any measure Shaw was a winner for Blount for many years.

However, Shaw became a considerable embarrassment for us in the 1980s, when the federal government instigated an extensive investigation of the fabricating industry. Two senior employees of Shaw as well as Shaw itself were convicted of charges related to an industrywide bid-rigging scheme. Both employees were sent to prison. No one else in Shaw was charged and no one in our corporate headquarters in Montgomery was charged. At my direction, we implemented a voluntary program of restitution to make customers whole. It cost millions, but it was the right thing to do.

The incident shook us up. It made me realize that we had many employees in positions of responsibility and authority who, if they conducted themselves in an unlawful or unethical manner, could lead to great embarrassment for the company. We installed a more extensive system of controls throughout the company, and we continue to monitor adherence for compliance not only for legal matters, but also for ethical issues.

MIXED BAG OF ACQUISITIONS

Shaw was acquired before I left for Washington. Now let me return to the subject of the acquisitions that were made while I was away. During that time, Blount bought a hodgepodge of businesses without any clear plan as to what it was trying to accomplish. There was no rhyme nor reason to them. They included a steel fabricating operation in Indiana and a mobile home company. There were others, mostly small companies, and just about every one of them was losing money. On returning to the company as chairman of the executive committee, I quickly concluded that a lot of damage had been done to Blount, and it did not take me long to decide to resume the presidency, which I did in January 1974. By 1979, I had sold or closed nearly all these acquired operations.

The worst of the operations was the mobile home company. In acquiring that company, Blount management lost sight of the principle, established in the Shaw acquisition, to look for the problems. The mobile home operation appeared to be making money — I stress the word appeared, because the previous owners had guaranteed

Opposite and above, Benjamin F. Shaw Company fabricated and installed piping systems for power plants, chemical and paper plants and oil refineries and was one of the largest mechanical contractors in the United States. Our 1967 purchase of Shaw established a pattern for future acquisitions.

substantial amounts of bank loans for the buyers of its homes. Blount inherited these liabilities. Even after we shut down the company, the loan guarantees had a very long tail: borrowers kept defaulting for years, and every time one of them did, we had to pay the bank and go after the borrower. We ended up losing $15 million in the mobile home business. It was a sorry chapter in Blount's history.

One of the few acquisitions from this period that did pay off was J. P. Burroughs & Sons of Saginaw, Michigan. Our merger with Burroughs took us into a new market, agribusiness. Equally important, through this transaction Blount became a public company. On July 11, 1972, merging with Burroughs, we acquired its 2,000 shareholders and became listed on the American Stock Exchange. We have been public ever since.

One reason I wanted to go public was that, of my five children, only two had any interest in working in the business. I felt that by going public I could deal more equitably with my children, giving each of them a liquid stock that they might eventually sell if they chose to do so. I also thought that being public would make Blount a better company, by forcing us to live by the discipline of issuing quarterly earnings reports, thereby shining a spotlight on the performance of management.

After acquiring Burroughs, we decided to operate in two distinct markets: construction and agribusiness. I felt we could use agribusiness as a core business to build around. Burroughs manufactured grain dryers, seed cleaners, roller mills and bucket elevators. (It was also at this time, in 1974, that we formed a holding company, Blount, Inc., to own our diverse operating units. We phased out the Blount Brothers Construction Company name and became Blount, Inc.) In 1976, we purchased Modern Farm Systems, which manufactured grain bins, metal farm buildings, tanks and related equipment. Other acquisitions followed in quick order, including York Foundry & Engine Works, which manufactured belt conveyors and bucket elevators; Redex Industries, which made dryers and grain-handling equipment; and Mix-Mill Manufacturing Company, which produced equipment to mix and grind feed for hogs, cattle and poultry.

Agribusiness became a sizable market for us. These various acquired companies had a total of 13 manufacturing plants, located primarily in the Midwest. By fiscal 1979, they were generating nearly half of Blount's operating income. In a speech that year I said, "We see tremendous potential in this market, not just in the United States, but in developing nations overseas, where we are concentrating major new market efforts in this growth segment of our company."

In 1976, we purchased Modern Farm Systems, which manufactured grain bins, metal farm buildings, tanks and related equipment. Modern Farm Systems was one of several acquisitions we made in agribusiness. At its peak in the late 1970s and early 1980s, agribusiness generated nearly half of Blount's operating income.

Several years later, agricultural markets went into a tailspin and we ended up divesting our agribusiness operations. Nonetheless, they had generated substantial profits for Blount for well over a decade.

WASHINGTON STEEL: A GREAT INVESTMENT

Continuing our diversification, in fiscal 1979 we made our largest acquisition up to that time, Washington Steel, adding a third leg to our company: specialty and stainless steels, in addition to construction and agribusiness.

Washington Steel was a wonderful company that brought us great good fortune. Headquartered in Washington, Pennsylvania, near Pittsburgh, it had production facilities in that state as well as in southern California. Following its acquisition, Blount's revenues increased to some $500 million annually; Washington Steel contributed about one-fifth of the total.

The acquisition of Washington Steel occurred in an unusual fashion. In 1979, we had just completed a major construction project at Tabuk, Saudia Arabia, and were flush with cash. Seeking to invest this money in an industrial company to support our diversification strategy, we screened various companies before arriving at a list of 20 candidates. Those 20 were then winnowed down to 10. Shortly thereafter, when we made a final cut to five, I received a phone call from my friend Peter Flanigan of Dillon Read, the Wall Street investment bank. He said his firm had been engaged to help Washington Steel fend off a hostile takeover bid, and he asked if I was interested in being a "white knight" in buying Washington Steel on a friendly basis — that is, with the support of its management. As it so happened, I knew of Washington Steel because it was one of our 20 candidates. I was indeed interested, even though it had not made our final cut. Peter warned, "There's a sense of urgency," to which I replied, "Why don't you get the chairman of Washington Steel down to our hunting lodge in Georgia this weekend and we'll talk."

Washington Steel's chairman was George Baumunk. Meeting with him that very weekend, I brought along two of our directors —

Bobby Radcliff and my brother Houston. The four of us had a ball riding horses and hunting, and in doing so George got to know us and we got to know him. George had not been on a horse or gone quail hunting in 20 years. I told Bobby and Houston to shoot with him, but give him credit for the birds that went down. Sunday afternoon, I invited George to return with me to Montgomery to talk business. We sat down that evening in the library of my home and negotiated a deal right there on the spot: Blount agreed to purchase Washington Steel for $61 million cash. (Earlier that same month, Shirley Milligan joined my staff as executive secretary. She's terrific. I told Bob Heaton, Washington Steel's number two man, that Shirley and Washington Steel were both great acquisitions, but Shirley was a lot less expensive. Shirley became my administrative assistant in the 1980s and my executive assistant in 1996. I rely on her tremendously in both my outside and company activities, as well as managing the Blount Corporate Collection of American Art.) Following the acquisition of Washington Steel, George stayed on as the company's president, subsequently being succeeded by Bob Heaton.

Opposite and below, Washington Steel specialized in the manufacture of stainless steel sheet, strip and plate. During our nine years of ownership, we modernized its facilities and improved its productivity nearly 40 percent. We were able to sell the company for more than four times our purchase price.

JOHN CONNALLY

Given Blount's growing presence in manufacturing, I wanted to broaden our corporate management team by adding an experienced executive as Blount's president and chief operating officer — someone who could oversee our manufacturing operations, would help train our future management and was approximately my own age. The third point was important, because I did not want our new president to develop a false expectation that he would succeed me as chairman and CEO. I also needed to strengthen our management team because I was once again active in politics, having taken on the national chairmanship of John Connally's presidential campaign in the 1980 Republican primaries. Tall, lean and good looking, John Connally was very charismatic. And he made stemwinder speeches. I first met John when President Nixon persuaded the face-card Democrat to become his secretary of treasury in 1971, just before Nixon's reelection in 1972. When John arrived in Washington, Secretary of State Bill Rogers, Secretary of Defense Mel Laird and I invited him to join us for a round of golf at the Congressional Club to welcome him to the cabinet. The next day we began to gather in the Cabinet Room awaiting the president, sitting around and talking. The president traditionally left the Oval Office and came through his secretary's office into the Cabinet Room, and we would all stop talking and stand while he came in. This particular morning, the first cabinet meeting which John Connally was to attend, the door burst open as if it were the president, and we all stood up. But it was John, coming in through the president's door. He was grinning like a Cheshire cat. No one said a word, and then I said, "John, you are the biggest ham in Washington." That broke the ice.

I first met Texas Governor John Connally when he joined the Nixon administration as treasury secretary in 1971. We became good friends and I headed his national campaign in the 1980 primaries for the Republican nomination for president. With his strong leadership skills and willingness to deal head-on with tough issues, I thought John would have been an excellent president.

John and I got to be good friends, and eight years later he asked me to be national chairman of his campaign. It was exciting, but very unproductive. John went around the country making truly great speeches and raising funds from the business community. We collected far more money than Ronald Reagan, George Bush or any of the others running for president in 1980.

Moreover, unlike many candidates, John was willing to address significant issues. We worked on a speech in which he made a clear break with existing policy on the Middle East. It was correct new policy, but controversial. A number of people, including Henry Kissinger and other Jewish leaders, read the speech and endorsed it.

However, as soon as John gave the speech, financial contributions to his campaign immediately dried up. All those who had embraced the speech began to fall away, and his campaign came to an end. He had won only a single delegate in the Republican primaries before pulling out. In retrospect, we had a face-card Democrat asking the Republican Party to give its highest honor to a recent Republican convert. There was no way that could be done.

OSCAR REAK

Meanwhile, as I said, I needed a strong executive to be president and chief operating officer of Blount. Through a headhunter, I found Oscar Reak, president of Cutler-Hammer, Inc., a company with sales comparable to those of Blount. Based in Milwaukee, Cutler-Hammer was a highly regarded manufacturer of electrical and electronic equipment. It had recently been acquired by Eaton Corporation — and, to our good fortune, Oscar was looking to get out. Oscar was a wonderful addition to our company. With his quiet self-confidence, ability to get along with people and willingness to tackle new manufacturing techniques, he made a major contribution to Blount over the next eight years. In addition, Oscar was very supportive and loyal. When he decided to retire at age 65, I persuaded him to stay two additional years. Even after he had retired, he came back when I needed him: at my request, he returned to serve as Blount president on an interim basis when his successor, Bill Van Sant, resigned unexpectedly. When Oscar was president of Blount, he ran our manufacturing business and I looked after our construction business, but we backed each other up, and this was the same way we operated when he

In 1979, we recruited Oscar Reak from Cutler-Hammer, a company similar in size to Blount, where he was president. We were drawn to Oscar by his proven abilities as a manufacturing executive. Oscar did a tremendous job as Blount's president and chief operating officer from 1979 to 1987. He watched over the manufacturing side of the business while I watched over construction. After retiring in 1987, he came back to serve as interim president when we needed him. Oscar is now retired and continues to live in the Montgomery area.

returned. He then retired for a second time, remaining on our board of directors until 1994. He is one of the nicest people in the world. I am grateful to him for his support.

Beginning with Oscar Reak, Blount has had three presidents: Oscar, Bill Van Sant and John Panettiere. John is now our CEO. Every one of the three has come from a manufacturing background.

With Oscar on board, we set out to increase Washington Steel's profits by reducing its costs. When we acquired Washington Steel, its managers told us the Japanese steel companies were killing them. They insisted the Japanese had modern equipment and new plants that made it almost impossible for Washington Steel to compete. Oscar and I took our people to Japan to see for ourselves, and we found that what our managers thought simply wasn't true. The Japanese plants and equipment were as old as ours. However, the Japanese knew how to run their plants better. They would take an old machine and upgrade it and put on the bells and whistles at far less cost than buying a new machine. And they would make small, important process improvements that our people hadn't even considered. The Japanese were doing a hundred little things better, and these various improvements added up to a significant competitive advantage

We set out to emulate the Japanese by improving our manufacturing processes and reducing our costs. We were very successful in this endeavor. When we acquired Washington Steel, it took 18 ½ man-hours to manufacture a ton of steel. Within a decade, we had trimmed that figure to 11 ½ hours. In 1983, in the middle of this complex and demanding process of productivity improvement and cost reduction, Washington Steel employees who were members of the United Steelworkers went on strike. In settling that strike, we were able to shift the employees' compensation toward an incentive arrangement — a concept I have long favored, dating back to the First Avenue Viaduct in 1949. In the settlement, the employees of Washington Steel agreed to a wage freeze at the 1983 level until 1991.

One magazine, taking note of this extraordinary concession by the employees, said it "made steel industry history." To compensate for the wage freeze, we established a profit-sharing plan with a unique twist: the plan was to last five years; however, in the year before it was to expire, employees had to vote whether they wanted to extend profit sharing beyond the five years or do away with it. And even if they voted to abolish profit sharing, wages would remain frozen until 1991. There was never any doubt what their choice would be. When the time came to decide, profit sharing had paid off handsomely for the employees, and they voted overwhelmingly to continue the arrangement. Profit sharing also benefited the company by aligning the interests of employees with those of Washington Steel. Because the employees' compensation was tied to profits, they worked harder and smarter and sought to control costs.

In 1988, nine years after we bought Washington Steel for $61 million, we sold it for $280 million. Although I liked Washington Steel and it was very profitable, we had a reason for selling it — but that's a story for a later chapter.

FIREWORKS AT LAKE MARTIN

The decade following my return from government service was not only a period of hard work and corporate change. I also found time to relax and have fun.

One of the singular episodes from this period occurred in 1975, the year before America's bicentennial. Figuring the bicentennial would be one of the great patriotic events of this century, I wanted to celebrate in an appropriate manner with my family, especially with my grandchildren, and I began to think about fireworks. I didn't want just a few Roman candles. I had a big fireworks show in mind. I wanted to stage it at our vacation home on Lake Martin, northeast of Montgomery. And just to make sure it met my every expectation, I decided to conduct a practice run in 1975.

I got a late start. On Tuesday morning, July 1, 1975 — just three days before the Fourth — I called Joe McInnes into my office and said, "Joe, do you know anything about fireworks?" Joe was a well-mannered young attorney who had joined our company a year earlier. Somehow, he survived the 1975 fireworks ordeal with all his fingers intact and is now a senior vice president of Blount. When I asked my question, Joe immediately replied, "Yes, sir." (As Joe recalled later, he didn't know anything about fireworks. But he was new to the company and didn't want to displease the boss.) I said, "I mean big fireworks, Joe." "Yes, sir" was again the response. So I said, "Look, Joe, I want these fireworks. I want big fireworks. And I want them on July Fourth at Lake Martin." "Yes, sir, no problem," he replied. I peeled off $2,000 of bills and handed them to Joe, directing him to spend the entire wad. He headed out the door and that was the last I saw of him until the Fourth.

Joe tells a very funny, deadpan version of what happened in the three days between July 1 and July 4. He left my office, closed the door behind him and leaned against the wall, his heart pumping like crazy. He wondered how in the world he had gotten himself into such a mess. Desperate, he called a friend, who told him the only person who could help was a fireworks dealer in Tennessee nicknamed Perk. Joe phoned Perk and explained his problem, to which Perk replied, "Son, that's impossible. It's too late. You have to have a federal permit, a state permit and a local permit." Joe was astonished, but insisted he had to put on a big fireworks display. He had no choice; the boss wanted it. Perk paused and said, "Well, it's impossible," but he told Joe to call someone named Carlton at the Bureau of Alcohol, Tobacco & Firearms in Atlanta about a federal permit.

Joe phoned Carlton, saying he had been referred by Perk. Carlton replied that any friend of Perk must be okay, and he told Joe to catch the next flight to Atlanta. A federal permit would be waiting. Arriving at the ATF, Joe was invited into Carlton's office. Carlton closed the door and asked, "Do you really know Perk?" Joe said he did, that he had talked with Perk that very morning. Carlton repeated that any friend of Perk had to be okay, and he issued a federal permit right then and there. Joe now had one permit, but needed two more. And he needed to buy the fireworks. He flew from Atlanta to Nashville, arriving on the evening of July 1 and staying in a hotel that night. Rising the next morning at the crack of dawn, he rented a station wagon and drove out to see Perk, the fireworks dealer. Joe proceeded to buy $2,000 worth of fireworks and load them into the back of the station wagon, whereupon Perk said, "Son, you can't drive that. It's like driving with three cases of dynamite in your car." Joe was undeterred. He said he had to do it because the boss wanted a fireworks show. Perk, wanting no part of the situation, reached into the back of the station wagon and eradicated his company's name from all the boxes. Literally taking his life into his hands, Joe headed for Montgomery in the station wagon, stopping in Birmingham for the night. The next morning, July 3rd, he drove to the capitol in Montgomery and showed his federal permit to the state fire marshall, who issued a state permit. Joe then headed north to Lake Martin, his station wagon still packed with fireworks, and obtained a local permit from the town fire department. He had accomplished the impossible! It has always been like that with Joe. He is straightforward and takes on challenges of all kinds, inside and outside the company. He has gone on to a very successful career at Blount and now serves as our senior vice president - administration and corporate secretary. He is also president of the Blount Foundation.

The next day was the Fourth. Joe and three of my sons, Winton, Tom and Sam, spent the better part of the afternoon putting the fireworks in place. The fireworks were launched from mortars — that is, by taking a firework, lighting its fuse, dropping it into the mortar and standing back as the projectile erupted out of the mortar toward the sky. That night, Joe and Winton put life and limb at risk, setting off the fireworks one by one as the rest of us watched from a safe distance. I still didn't know anything about Joe's harrowing adventure. All I knew was that I was delighted with the results. And so were my grandchildren.

A few days later, Joe wrote me a letter that said, "Dear Mr. Blount, I don't know what you think of your children, but Mr. McInnes thinks a lot of me. I suggest you get a professional to do this next year." Joe subsequently told me the whole story. We have used a professional ever since.

From that unbelievable and unforgettable beginning, my annual fireworks show has become a fixture on Lake Martin. What started out as a family affair for the grandchildren has turned into the largest Fourth of July fireworks display in the state of Alabama. Each year, we hire a team of professionals from Pennsylvania to detonate $25,000 worth of fireworks in 30 minutes. Boats packed with spectators fill the southern end of Lake Martin, and the bridge across the lake is jammed with thousands more on foot (the highway patrol closes the bridge to vehicles). All told, an estimated 20,000 to 25,000 people take in the action.

As for me, I would like to take my wife, Carolyn, to Wimbledon for the All-England tennis tournament, which is held at the beginning of July. But I can't because of the fireworks show. Of course, I enjoy giving it, and it offers a chance to see my children and grandchildren and throw a big party for my family and friends. But it's become so popular, I couldn't stop now even if I wanted to.

A big fireworks show is more complicated than you ever imagined.

CHAPTER SEVEN

The $2 Billion
Saudi Project

THE YEAR 1973 SAW A QUADRUPLING OF WORLD oil prices and, with it, a massive transfer of global wealth to the Middle East. Flush with cash, the Middle Eastern oil-producing nations began to invest huge sums in the modernization of infrastructure — everything from hospitals to military bases to universities to petrochemical plants. Capitalizing on this opportunity, we opened offices in Beirut, Teheran and Riyadh and started bidding on work.

The Middle East turned out to be a major source of profits for Blount for more than a decade, culminating in our construction of the $2 billion King Saud University, the world's largest fixed-price construction contract up to that time — and by far the most profitable single project in the history of Blount.

We did very well in the Middle East, especially in Saudi Arabia. But we also had a few setbacks. We were run out of Beirut when the Lebanese civil war erupted in 1975. As a result, we never did build anything in that beleaguered country.

I speak with personal sadness about Lebanon, because I saw for myself the awful devastation. In the 1980s, I went to Beirut at the request of President Reagan. He asked me to head a committee of contractors and financiers who visited Lebanon to evaluate how the United States might help rebuild that nation's infrastructure if and when the opportunity arose. Our group arrived during a lull in the fighting. Even though the once-elegant city of Beirut ("the Paris of

Opposite, two arched walkways at right angles to each other — one a mile long, the other five-eighths of a mile long — form the spine of King Saud University. All the individual colleges are connected by these walkways. Left, a Saudi guard at the construction site. Our workforce came from nearly 30 countries and spoke nearly 100 dialects, presenting a monumental challenge of coordination and control.

the Middle East") was in ruins, the people were energetic and resourceful. Beirut looked like one of those bombed-out German cities following World War II. Yet, we found a little shop which a Lebanese buinessman had opened in the midst of the devastation and rubble. For me, this shop came to symbolize the resilience and optimism of the Lebanese people. In our talks with the Lebanese, we constantly heard the conviction that their country could be reconstructed with a minimum of outside money. They were not seeking significant American help in this regard. What they needed most, they said, was peace and security. Our committee reported back to President Reagan that there wasn't anything America could do until the fighting stopped.

MAJOR PROJECTS IN IRAN

Blount was very successful in Iran... until the revolution. We were building four projects, including an addition to the Sheraton Hotel in Teheran and a resort on the Caspian Sea, as well as a housing project in southern Iran, when we were forced out by the 1979 revolution that brought Ayatollah Khomeini to power. We were still owed $11 million when we left. We agreed to a settlement of $2 million out of $7 million due on our largest claim and probably would not have collected much on our remaining claims. But then the Iranians reneged even on the $2 million. So we took our case to a tribunal set up to adjudicate American claims against Iran and eventually collected a total of just over $7 million including interest!

I did not meet the shah when we were doing business in Iran. However, a few months after he was overthrown, I was visiting my brother, Houston, who had a home in Cuernavaca, Mexico, where the shah was living. The shah was a good friend of both President Nixon

One of our contracts in Iran was to build housing in Bushire on the Arabian Gulf coast. Terry Honan, who headed our Iranian operations, is third from the right in this photograph. The project was 98 percent complete when we were driven out of Iran by the revolution.

and Admiral Thomas Moorer, the retired chairman of the Joint Chiefs of Staff who was a member of Blount's board of directors. Of course, I knew President Nixon, and Tom and I had become fast friends. So I sent word to the shah that I would enjoy having an opportunity to meet him, and he invited me over. We talked for at least two hours. He was filled with rage toward President Carter. He said, "You know, your president called me almost daily about calming the troops. And I would tell my generals, 'Go back to the barracks and calm the troops.' Now the generals have been murdered one by one." He asked me, "What is America going to do about that?" The shah recalled that his government had thousands of tanks and other military equipment. He needed these armaments, he said, to keep order in the Middle East and stand in the way of the Russians if they decided to invade to the south. He asked me how many troops President Carter would send to replace this military might. The United States had turned its back on a valued ally — with the stupidity of the Carter administration's foreign policy (the shah and I agreed on that point). He was convinced he could have crushed the revolution in three days if the United States had given him free rein to do so. He said it might have meant killing two or three thousand people, but that was peanuts compared to what was happening. I left shaking my head not only over the bitterness of this once-mighty monarch but also over the shortsightedness of United States policy.

SUCCESS IN SAUDI ARABIA

Despite our mixed results elsewhere in the Middle East, in Saudi Arabia we hit a home run. We began by running practice bids — that is, calculating bids, but not submitting them, to see how our bids compared with those of our competitors. One of the complicating factors in Saudi Arabia was the shortage of port facilities, adding greatly to the costs of importing construction materials. The harbors were jam-packed, and ships sometimes had to wait as long as six months to unload. The demurrage you had to pay each day for a ship's waiting to unload was astronomical.

After running a number of practice bids, we won our first Saudi contract in 1976, to build a military base at Tabuk near the Red Sea, not far from the Israeli and Jordanian borders. It was a sizable job, about $150 million. The Middle East is a ticklish place to do business. It is very relationship oriented; knowing the right people and gaining their respect is essential, as it is almost anywhere. I started getting reports that the Tabuk project was not going well, so I went to Saudi Arabia and confirmed for myself that we were falling behind.

W. E. "Bull" Wilson joined
Blount in 1960 and spent the
next 36 years with us, retiring in 1996. He handled
some of our most challenging construction projects
and is the best project manager we ever had.

Our first project in Saudi
Arabia was at Tabuk, in the
middle of the desert, where
we built a military base.
One of our biggest tasks was
to produce our own gravel,
concrete and concrete
block. It was not like projects in the United States,
where you buy those mate-
rials from others.

If we messed up that first job, it's doubtful we ever would have
received another assignment in Saudi Arabia.

John Caddell had succeeded Paul Hess as president of our construction division in the late 1960s and did an outstanding job. John
is a feisty fellow and very smart. He has a great sense of the construction business. Estimating and analyzing are his long suits, and he
hangs very tough on negotiations. As soon as I was aware of the problems at Tabuk, I phoned John in the United States and said, "I want
Bull Wilson over here right away." Bull Wilson was our best project
manager, perhaps the best in the construction industry. If you were
to meet Bull, you might think he was one of the roughest, toughest
persons in the world. He played halfback for Auburn University in
the late 1940s. He's built like a brick wall and is still in great shape. He
is also well educated, very smart and extremely capable. No matter
what the assignment, I have always been able to count on Bull to take
charge and get it done right. In addition, he is a real character and
loves to tell funny stories about me, some of which are true. We're
good pals. In our earlier years we used to do things like hand
wrestling, but no longer!

Bull straightened out the Tabuk job in no time, and it ended up
being very profitable for Blount. The successful completion of the
Tabuk job was, no doubt, a key for us when we became interested in
the $2 billion King Saud University project.

Incidentally, Bull took a liking to the Middle East and kept
working there until he retired in 1996, in the final years heading our
last projects in Kuwait. With his bigger-than-life personality and
ability to manage any project, he has become a construction industry
legend in that region of the world.

The Tabuk project was being supervised by the U.S. Corps of
Engineers. Bull and the contracting officer, Colonel Milton Lee

Little, became friends. I also became friendly with Colonel Little, and we played tennis several times when I visited the job — but we always had to wait until sundown because of the intense heat, between 110 and 120 degrees Fahrenheit, during the day. After he left the military, Colonel Little remained in Saudi Arabia for several years working on various projects. I guess the Middle East got into his blood, as it did with Bull.

Whiskey is not allowed in Saudi Arabia, which posed a problem for numerous foreign companies and their personnel. Just before I arrived, the Saudi religious police had raided the compound of a company which was running the hospital on the base at Tabuk where we were working. One of the British doctors had some liquor and was arrested. Justice moves swiftly in Saudi Arabia: two days after being arrested, the doctor was sentenced to two years in jail. Back then, conditions in Saudi jails were unbelievably bad. The doctor's wife was shipped off to England.

My son, Sam Blount, worked on the Tabuk job and was living with his wife at that time, Jane, in the Blount compound. Jane was pregnant and later returned to the United States to have their baby, my granddaughter, Kelly Blount, who was born on my birthday, February 1st, as was another granddaughter, Stuart Blount Massey. I thought what had happened to the British doctor would have gotten everybody's attention. But when I visited Sam and Jane in their living quarters, I discovered that the bathtubs were filled with large bottles of homemade white and red wine. I yelled at Sam to get that stuff out of there. Sam poured the red wine down the drain, but I learned much later that he kept the white wine for some time. There was nothing I could have done if he had been caught. I still cringe at the idea.

The military base at Tabuk included housing and a hospital. Here, workers erect an exterior wall. If we had not completed the Tabuk project on time, we never would have been given the opportunity to bid on the huge King Saud University project.

This hard hat has witnessed a great deal of Blount history. Bull Wilson bought it in 1961 for $4.60 at a hardware store in Dothan, Alabama, where we were building several schools, and wore it on jobs for the next 14 years.

MY ILLNESS IN SAUDI ABRABIA. . . AND A DECISION THAT CHANGED MY LIFE

When I first heard the details of the Saudis' planned new university on the outskirts of Riyadh, I knew it was right up Blount's alley. We eventually won the contract to build this one-of-a-kind project and it turned out to be a fascinating job, but with many unexpected twists and turns along the way.

One of the unusual aspects is that it took us longer (four years) to negotiate the final contract, because of difficulties in pinning down all the details with the Saudis, than it did to build the university (40 months) once the contract was approved.

Moreover, the amount of the down payment, $343 million, was so large we had a courier hand-carry the check on the Concorde supersonic transport from Bahrain to London to New York, and then by helicopter from JFK Airport to Morgan Guaranty Trust Company in lower Manhattan, so we could draw interest on the money the next day. You would have done the same when you realized the interest on that check was almost $200,000 daily. Short-term interest rates had just peaked at 20 percent. Carolyn said she never thought she'd live to see the day when I sang the praises of high interest rates. How sweet they were!

Through this project, I made many friends in Saudi Arabia and learned about the culture. Saudi Arabia is one of the most prosperous and modern nations in the Middle East. It is also one of the most exotic and beautiful. Traveling through the desert with Arab friends, sleeping in a tent

We received a down payment of more than $343 million on the King Saud University project. We rushed the check by courier from Saudi Arabia to New York so we could deposit it in our bank and begin earning interest as quickly as possible. That interest came to nearly $200,000 a day! I still keep a copy of the check, encased in plastic, on my desk.

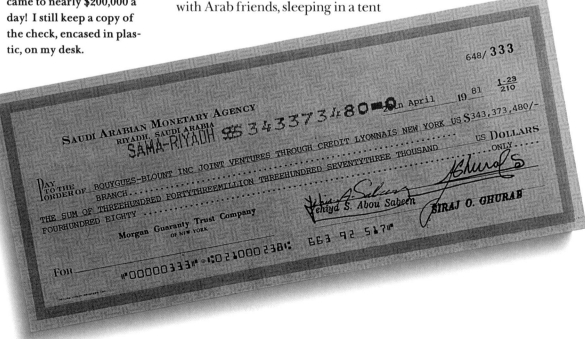

under a canopy of stars glistening more brightly in the crisp desert air than you could possibly imagine, is an extraordinary experience.

But there also came a time in Saudi Arabia when my health failed me, a harrowing experience that changed my life. It occurred on one of my early trips to Riyadh, the Saudi capital. My brother, Houston, who was then chairman and CEO of Vulcan Materials, was also in Saudi Arabia at that time. He had taken Vulcan to Saudi to produce aggregates. He visited me in Riyadh for breakfast, and we made arrangements to play tennis on a court in the compound of a Saudi prince who was a friend of mine. As we were eating breakfast, suddenly my tongue got thick and I could not complete sentences or say words correctly. There was great confusion as Houston tried to find a doctor and hospital. Later that morning, as I began to speak a little more coherently, Houston and I began talking about my will. He got Tom Carruthers, my lawyer, on the phone from Birmingham, Alabama, and we updated my will just in case. We also talked about who might take over as CEO of Blount, Inc. It was a calm discussion, but prudent. Houston and I never did get to play tennis.

The doctors ended up putting me in a tent in a small U.S. Army medical unit in Riyadh. They began a series of tests and for a number of days could not agree what had happened to me. They thought it was a stroke or maybe a heart attack. We had been in touch with the University of Alabama (UAB) Medical School in Birmingham, and when my heart rate subsided, they put me on a plane to UAB. After numerous tests, about 10 days later the doctors at UAB determined I had kidney cancer and they removed my left kidney. Fortunately, the cancer was encapsulated and they took it all out, and I have not had any recurrence of this condition, which was 15 years ago as I write this.

That whole episode got me thinking about how I wanted to live the rest of my life. I had let my joy in my work mask so many things. It was clear to me that I had a very unhappy marriage, and the marital tensions were beginning to affect our children. It was also clear that I cared very much for Carolyn Varner. I had asked her to marry me in the 1960s. We both had young children at that time and Carolyn had said she thought it would be too traumatic for them if their parents divorced. But in 1980, Carolyn got a divorce, and when I recovered from my kidney cancer, I then got a divorce, and we were married December 22, 1981. It was a glorious day. Joy flooded into our lives, and the last 15 years have been deliriously happy with a growing love and a wonderful partnership. There has been no greater event in my life than my marriage to Carolyn. It has changed me enormously, opening a whole new world and a whole new way of life.

My marriage to Carolyn Varner on December 22, 1981, brought incredible joy into my life. Love like ours doesn't just happen in fairy tales. Our devotion to each other has only grown stronger with time.

A MEMORABLE JOURNEY THROUGH THE DESERT π

As I stated earlier, personal relationships count far more in the Middle East than in other countries. Mixing business and pleasure is part of the culture. I developed a great respect and fondness for Dr. Monsour Al Turki, president of King Saud University (KSU). When he came to the United States with his wife and young children to visit Disney World, I invited them to spend a few days with us in Montgomery. His lovely wife, Moniere, is highly educated and speaks several languages, including English. She and Carolyn became good friends. When I told Dr. Al Turki that Carolyn and I were getting married, he invited us to Saudi Arabia for our honeymoon. He said we would go out into the desert and stay in tents, and that traveling in the Saudi desert was much like going down the white waters of the Colorado River.

After talking it over, Carolyn and I accepted his gracious offer. We started our honeymoon in Bermuda at the Coral Beach Club, where we met Carol and Bill Bailey on the tennis court. Bill was president of Aetna Insurance. We remain friends with the Baileys today, sometimes meeting them at the home of a mutual friend, Jerry Hudson, in Maine. Jerry had become Blount's bonding agent, representing Aetna, after the death of John Overton, and he and I have developed a great friendship.

From Bermuda, Carolyn and I went to Vail, Colorado, where I had been skiing since 1969. Although Carolyn was not a skier, she knew the sport was very important to me and agreed to try it for two

Oral history is part of Saudi culture. In this way, more than through books, each generation is taught the story of the Saudi people. Here, Carolyn and I spend a fascinating evening listening to oral history. The man to my right is an interpreter.

years. I got Howard Rapson, my ski instructor, to give her some lessons. Carolyn had a fear of heights. That first day, I was going down the slope with her when we came to a drop. She started shaking and couldn't move. I held her closely, but she wouldn't turn loose. We eventually got to the bottom. A few days later, we went to Davos, Switzerland, where I was attending the European World Forum meeting, and then to St. Anton, Austria. I asked for a ski instructor at St. Anton, and we were introduced to Pepi Groebel. Pepi and his brother were world champion skiers in the late '40s and '50s. He was about my age, 61, at the time. He told Carolyn he had taught Queen Wilhelmina, Maria von Trapp and Jackie Kennedy how to ski, and now he was going to teach "Princess Carolyn." That remark got them off to a great start, and soon she was skiing down the slopes with confidence. When we returned to Vail a month or so later, we went up the lift with my instructor, Howard Rapson. He told Carolyn to make a turn or two once we got off the lift and then wait for us. She said, "No, Howard, you and Red ski down the mountain a way and wait for me." Howard gave me a surprised look, and we went on down. Carolyn followed, making smooth turns, and stopped right by us, throwing a little snow on our skis. Howard said, "What the hell is this?" That week Howard took her down two of the most difficult slopes and the ski school put her picture on the front page of the *Vail Trail* paper, naming her "skier of the week." From there, it's been all downhill. She loves skiing, just as I do.

After this second visit to Vail, we flew to Saudi Arabia. Arriving in Riyadh, I left Carolyn at the Marriott Hotel and went to see Dr. Al Turki to discuss the details of our desert journey. He said we would leave Riyadh in automobiles the next morning and drive $5\frac{1}{2}$ hours through the desert to his father-in-law's farm, northwest of the Saudi capital. Our party was to include a number of department heads at KSU, as well as Dr. Al Turki's father-in-law, who was 80, and the father-in-law's brother, 85. It dawned on me he had not mentioned his wife. When we were invited, I thought there would just be two couples — Dr. Al Turki and his wife and Carolyn and me. Instead, the party consisted of 20 men and Carolyn. When I returned to the hotel and told her, she started having second thoughts. But we went and had a great time. The next day, as we were driving through the desert, Dr. Al Turki suddenly said it was time to stop for tea. Carolyn and I hadn't noticed, but our entourage was being followed by a car filled with Bedouins. We went up quite high into the sand dunes and the Bedouins piled out of their car, bringing up Arabian rugs and gold and silver tea service. Carolyn, Dr. Al Turki and I sat on the rugs drinking tea, looking down at the asphalt road winding through the desert. It was a breathtaking sight. I had bought a new camera before we left the United States, and I started taking pictures of this once-in-a-lifetime scene. Because I have never been very good with cameras, I had bought one that was as automatic as could be. I took more pictures the next day. But when I opened the camera to change the film, I discovered it was empty. I had bought the most foolproof camera in the world — and had forgotten to put in the film!

The ranch owned by Dr. Al Turki's father-in-law and his brother measured 150 by 80 kilometers, roughly the size of the state of Connecticut. In addition to raising sheep, they raised wheat for domestic consumption in Saudi Arabia, with some left over for export. The ranch had an ancient irrigation system. But in the middle of the ranch was a modern center-point irrigation system which you find in the United States and is considered state-of-the-art. Rivers flow beneath the sands of Saudi Arabia. In fact, much of the water for Riyadh, a city of well over one million inhabitants, comes from these underground rivers and in some cases is piped several hundred miles to the city.

After our honeymoon, I took Carolyn with me on all my trips to Saudi Arabia. The Saudis did not like the idea, but I stuck to my guns and took her anyway. One aspect of Saudi culture that is difficult for Americans to comprehend is the near-total subservience of women. Early on, Dr. Al Turki's wife invited Carolyn to tea at their home. Carolyn visited the Blount compound to get information about local

Below, Carolyn and I learned to ride camels on our trips into the desert. Opposite, I wrote my name in sand in the Saudi desert, but the wind soon swept it away.

dos and don'ts before she went. She did not want to make any mistakes in a very disciplined culture. She was told not to discuss religion or women's liberation. There were nine Saudi women at the tea, sitting on cushions around a large circular table. Four of the Saudi women spoke English and their first question was, "Tell us about your Jesus." The second was, "Tell us about women's liberation." To the first, Carolyn told them how she loved Jesus and why. Their response was, "We love your Jesus, too. He is the only prophet to go to Heaven alive." As to the second question, Carolyn threw up her hands and said, "I know nothing about women's liberation."

In Saudi Arabia, women are not allowed to drive, so Carolyn needed a chauffeur. Although visiting women are not required to wear veils, all women must wear black abayas that cover their legs down to the ankles as well as their arms and their necks. In Riyadh, we saw a number of German ladies in the supermarket wearing shorts. The religious police arrived and started flicking their bare legs with switches. They then arrested them and made their husbands come to the jail, whereupon they arrested the husbands and let the women go. They proceeded to give long lectures to the husbands about how to control wives. Carolyn and I never had any problems and we loved the people. Carolyn wore a black abaya whenever she went out. It is the Saudis' country, and we believed we should abide by their laws and respect their customs, even if they were not our own customs.

I said earlier that it took four years to negotiate the contract for KSU and only 40 months to build the university. There were many reasons for the protracted negotiations, not the least of which was that the Saudis are tough bargainers. Of course, I am too.

We had many thorny issues to resolve before construction could begin on the project. One related to Blount's financial liability for the project. We bid through a subsidiary, seeking to shield Blount, Inc., from liability in the event something went wrong. If the project lost money, our subsidiary might go belly up, but Blount would not. However, the Saudis objected. They insisted Blount, Inc., guarantee the project, putting our entire company at risk. Oscar Reak, who joined Blount as president in the middle of these negotiations, said, "We'll never agree to that. I'll be dead in my grave before we do." And the Blount board of directors questioned me strongly on whether we really wanted to put the entire company on the line. But we had to do so if we wanted the project — and I felt the profit potential was simply too great to pass up. So we did what the Saudis demanded: Blount, Inc., guaranteed the project. Tom Carruthers, our counsel, called it a "bet-the-company" decision. It was a bet-the-company decision that paid off handsomely.

As contract negotiations got under way, the Saudis began to scale down the project, and this too complicated the negotiations. Their original plan, on which we had bid, called for a huge university that would attract young people from across the Middle East. They envisioned 40,000 students, equal to the largest universities in the United States. However, the Iranian revolution made them nervous about letting thousands of young people into their country from other nations in the Middle East, and they cut back to 25,000 students — still impressive, but nothing like 40,000.

Because of this change, and because the Saudi government felt our original bid was too high, we negotiated for months on price. It was ironic that they thought our price was steep; our original bid of $3.5 billion was, in fact, $1 billion below the next-nearest competitor. We certainly didn't think we were overcharging. Nonetheless, some reduction of our original bid was justified by the reduced scale of the project, but just how much was hotly debated.

John Caddell headed our management team on the project, including the negotiations, and did an excellent job. However, as the negotiations dragged on, I became involved and was continuously involved until the project was completed and the final payment was made.

We had many bargaining sessions in Riyadh. The Saudi negotiating team was led by Dr. Al Turki. A graduate of Michigan State, he is bright and gracious and has a lively sense of humor. The Saudis were always dressed in traditional Arab robes. In addition, it was their custom at our negotiating sessions to serve tea or coffee. Saudi tea, if you haven't tasted it, is very bitter and takes some getting used to. Among our people, I started referring to the length of the negotiating sessions by the number of cups of tea I had to consume. Most memorable was a protracted, 10-cup-of-tea parley at which all hell broke loose. There was a dispute over contract terms, and I felt the Saudis were being unreasonable. No longer able to contain my anger, I slammed my fist on the table and declared, "We're not going to stand for this. We're leaving right now." There was dead silence as I gathered my papers and led my negotiating team to the Blount compound. Many of our people were nervous, wondering what would happen next. I said, "We're not going to give in. We're going to stay right here and sit tight." Half an hour later, Dr. Al Turki arrived at our compound. He came

into our office in his flowing robes and walked back to where I was working. He and I sat and talked, and he asked me to return to the negotiations, which I did.

To help move the negotiations along, I developed what I called the "10-10 rule." The Saudis wanted to know what this meant. I explained that if they wanted us to trim our price by 10 percent, they had to agree to a 10 percent reduction in the scope of the work. Such a formula may sound simplistic. However, the Saudis accepted the idea, and it enabled both sides to quell their emotions and reach an agreement without worrying about losing face by giving in. Sometimes the most obvious solution is the best solution.

We signed the contract and began construction in April 1981, four years after having submitted our original bid. The agreed-on price was $2 billion.

Dr. Monsour Al Turki was the president of King Saud University. He was determined to open the new university on schedule, and his ability to make quick decisions helped facilitate the timely completion of the project. Dr. Al Turki is not only extremely bright, but he also has a wonderful sense of humor. We have remained friends and still talk on occasion by phone.

There is another aspect of the Saudi project to which I have not yet referred: our alliance with Bouygues, the French contractor.

When the Saudis first asked for bids, perhaps a dozen contractors qualified. We were among them and wanted to bid by ourselves. However, in pre-qualifying companies, the Saudi government aligned them into four separate groups, like arranged marriages, and suggested that the members of each group bid jointly. Apparently they were concerned whether any single contractor could manage the project on its own. They recommended we bid jointly with Bouygues, and we did just that.

We had to negotiate all the items of the bid with Bouygues, and for the most part that went well. However, we took a 45 percent stake in the alliance to Bouygues' 55 percent, and this arrangement caused us no end of grief, even though we had valid reasons at the time for accepting a minority position. The Foreign Corrupt Practices Act and the Anti-Boycott Act had just been passed by the U.S. Congress, imposing draconian penalties on American companies that violated these laws. Because the laws were brand-new, our attorneys advised, rightly so, that their interpretation and enforcement were unclear. While we had no intention of violating the law, and we made clear to

We set up this office in downtown Riyadh when we first started bidding on projects in Saudi Arabia. Our work in the Middle East helped drive Blount's results for nearly a decade.

Bouygues that they must not either and made them sign such an agreement in the contract, the best way to protect ourselves was by taking a minority position. In this way, we hoped we would not be responsible for Bouygues' actions as majority partner. If we had been majority owner, we might well have been responsible. We never had a single problem with either of these laws, but at the time being extra cautious was the best thing to do.

Once the project got under way, we had endless disputes with our partner. Bouygues respected our employees on the construction site, because these employees knew their jobs and were more experienced than the Bouygues people. However, from a project management viewpoint, there was constant bickering. Although our people essentially built the job, Bouygues retained the final say in everything. And many of their choices were, in my view, misinformed or ill-advised. For instance, we subcontracted certain work to Holzman, a German firm, with the concurrence of Bouygues. Bouygues later repudiated that arrangement, and it took three years to get Bouygues' approval to pay Holzman for its work. I am certain that another subcontracting arrangement made by Bouygues resulted in $15 million of unnecessary expense.

To make matters worse, I did not get along with Francis Bouygues, chairman and chief executive officer of the Bouygues company. I thought he was a bully who tried to run over our people. I had a meeting with Francis Bouygues in London at the Connaught Hotel. Oscar Reak was with me and Bouygues had his No. 2 man, Rene Augereau, who was very reasonable, and he and I got along fine and later worked well together. At this meeting in London, Carolyn was in one room of the suite and we four men were in an adjoining room discussing some issues on the job. Carolyn said she cracked the door and looked into the negotiating room. Francis Bouygues and I were sitting at a small table with only about a foot between our heads. Bouygues started screaming, "I am Bouygues, I am Bouygues." He was completely out of control. Then I started saying, "I am Blount, I am Blount."

One night, at the height of the tensions between the two organizations, Bull Wilson got up at a Blount party and addressed all of our people. "I know you hate the French," he said. "I know you have good reason." Then he paused for a moment and said, "What do we gain by fighting them?" He said the important point was to complete the project successfully and on time. He had this large audience of Blount employees in the palm of his hand. When he finished, they gave him a standing ovation. That's Bull Wilson — smart, capable, takes charge, does not lose sight of what's important.

The project itself was huge and complex by any standard. Bull Wilson says it was like building 20 skyscrapers in midtown Manhattan all at once.

Foremost was the task of putting together a team of qualified people on the other side of the world from our corporate headquarters in Montgomery. At the height of construction, 12,500 workers from nearly 30 countries were on the project, and they spoke nearly 100 different dialects. Although we had interpreters working alongside them, it was a nightmare of coordination and control.

The university encompassed 6.8 million square feet of building space housing eight colleges, a student center, a two-million-book library, an administration building, a media center with two performing arts theaters, a dining hall and a mosque.

As part of the project, we built 18 electrical substations within the university. There were more than 100,000 individual electrical fixtures; it took an entire year's output from a plant in the United States to manufacture them. We installed nearly 6,000 miles of electrical cable.

We installed 3,700 tons of structural steel and 27,000 tons of rebar.

The construction site was outside Riyadh in the desert. Because there was no existing infrastructure, we built seven plants on-site to produce the required 520,000 cubic yards of concrete.

We also built a precast plant that manufactured 76,000 precast elements.

The Saudis are so concerned about explosives we had to have representatives of the police, the military and the government on site each time we wanted to blast.

A truck arrived every 12 seconds on average, posing a monumental challenge in traffic management.

We also had to be sensitive to local customs. For instance, we used Turks to build the mosque because they are Muslims.

The whole job was just massive and intricate in every conceivable way.

Our people and their spouses lived in a compound we built on the site of KSU. The compound had a number of recreation facilities, such as a swimming pool and tennis courts. But the numbing constant heat wore everybody down, and with very little contact with outsiders, it was a difficult experience for our people. Carolyn and I, on our visits to the job site, always hosted a party in downtown Riyadh, and we would have the wives and husbands dress up for fun and frolic, but without wine and whiskey. All our people looked forward to these parties. Carolyn would gather the wives together, along with the French wives some of the time, and she would speak to the group in French, telling all the ladies who were thousands of miles from home how much we admired and appreciated the sacrifices they were making, and how important they were to keeping up the morale of their husbands, who were working 12 to 18 hours a day. She also told them they would remember their time in Saudi Arabia the rest of their lives — and in fact, the successful completion of the job would serve to unite the families in shared experiences. They loved it. It was a break in the difficult times they were going through.

The Saudis wanted to build their new university as quickly as possible, and we agreed to do so in just 40 months. It is a tribute to our people that we met the schedule, completing the project in August 1984. We succeeded because we had a well-honed group of managers who knew what they were doing, and worked extremely hard to meet our goals. And we paid great attention to detail. We were confident going into the project, and that confidence was justified.

Not many people will have the opportunity to do what we did. It was a wonderful experience for all of us at Blount. We built one of the most beautiful universities in the world right on time in 40 months. It is a magnificent facility. I felt like a proud papa at the dedication.

As the project was nearing completion, I went to Riyadh to give a speech to 900 prominent Saudis in the university auditorium, which was one of the first buildings to be opened. On my way to the auditorium, I visited with Dr. Al Turki in his office. He was wearing a "talking" wristwatch that told the current temperature and humidity. I had never seen a watch like that before. So I asked him about it, and he took it off and gave it to me. In Saudi Arabia, if you admire someone's necktie, they'll give it to you. But, you have to give them yours in return. So, when Dr. Al Turki gave me his watch, I put it on my wrist and took off my watch and gave it to him. When I entered the auditorium, Carolyn and my son, Winton, were sitting toward the front of the audience. As I was about to begin my speech, out of the corner of my eye I caught them laughing and pointing to their wrists, obviously trying to tell me something. Unbeknownst to me, my new watch had started talking, and it was being picked up by the microphone. Everybody in the hall kept hearing the latest temperature and humidity. The kicker to the story is that I got back to the United States and found you could buy that same "talking" wristwatch for $29. On the other hand, the watch I had given to Dr. Al Turki cost $1,000. However you look at it, I did not come out well on that deal.

With an enrollment of 25,000 students, King Saud University is one of the largest universities in the Middle East and rivals the size of many large public universities in the United States. Its 6.8 million square feet of building space house eight colleges, a student center, a two-million-book library, an administration center, a media center with two performing arts theaters, a dining hall and a mosque.

All of the columns and
overhead elements in this
picture are made of precast
concrete. We built our own
concrete plant at the King
Saud University site and
made all the precast ele-
ments ourselves. The large
horizontal piece, approximately one-third of the way
from the top of the picture,
weighs 31 tons and is the
largest single precast ele-
ment on the project.

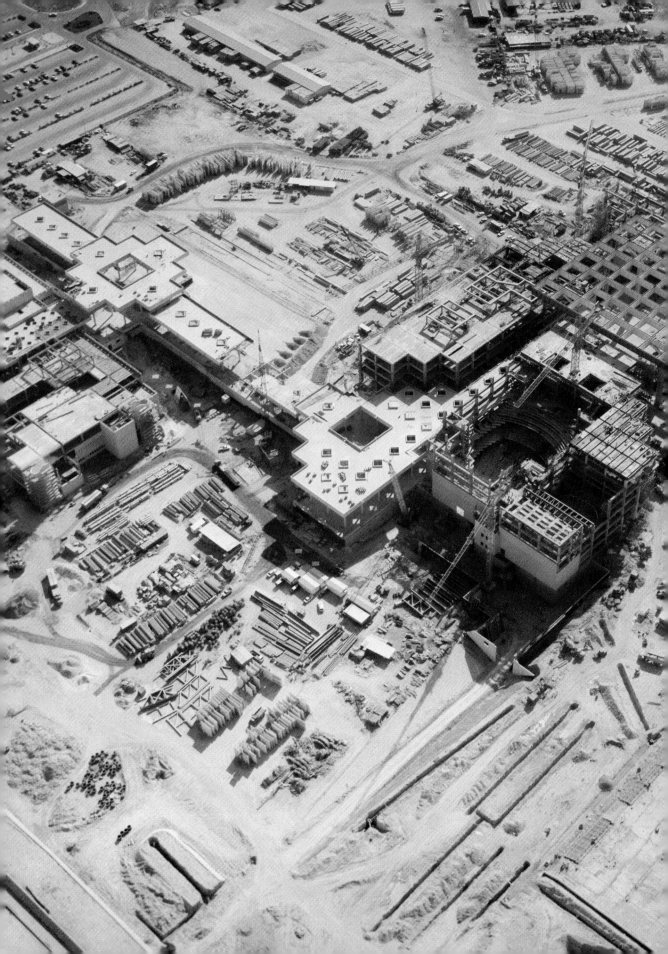

This photograph shows the full sweep of the 1,600-acre King Saud University campus. We had to build the entire university in just 40 months from the ground up on what had been barren desert. Missing the August 1984 deadline for completion would have been a nightmare, since a full contingent of students was already enrolled to begin classes that fall. Because of the beauty and size of the facility, and because we performed so well in meeting an incredibly tight deadline, King Saud University is one of the projects of which I am most proud.

After the university was completed, we had a terrible time settling the contract. The Saudis, tough bargainers as always, kept coming up with all kinds of reasons why they couldn't pay us the final six percent — the not inconsiderable sum of $120 million. Legitimately, we had about a year's worth of additional fine-tuning on the job, but even after that was completed the Saudis refused to pay. They would say that a floor in such-and-such a building needed additional work and excuses like that. Finally, it got ridiculous.

In 1988, I went to Saudi Arabia with Rene Augereau, vice chairman of Bouygues, to negotiate a final settlement. We agreed to accept $45 million in lieu of the $120 million. The Saudis, in turn, agreed to wipe out all their claims. However, once that deal was closed, the Saudis would not even pay the $45 million! They just kept stalling. I felt like I was on a never-ending merry-go-round.

After a time, I talked with Larry Eagleburger, U.S. deputy secretary of state, whom I knew from my days in Washington. He contacted the American ambassador to Saudi Arabia, who talked with the Saudi finance minister. They had interminable meetings, but the ambassador always came back with no answers.

In 1991, I finally went to my friend, Prince Bandar, the Saudi ambassador to the United States. Prince Bandar had been a pilot in the Saudi Air Force, and several years earlier had trained at the Air University in Montgomery. I knew him from his days in Alabama. He agreed to look into the matter. A few weeks later, he got back to me and said he felt we were entitled to more than the $45 million and would try to arrange that we receive the full amount we deserved. However, he then ran into the reality that we had already agreed to accept $45 million. He said the Saudi government was locked into the maximum of $45 million, but he did promise to get that amount. True to his word, the first half came in early 1993, nearly nine years after we had completed the project. I went personally to

The university's central courtyard is called the Forum. The roof was especially difficult to construct. It is 100 feet above the ground and was built in place, slightly higher than it is now, supported by temporary shoring. Once the roof was completed, we lowered it as a single unit onto four columns, one at each corner, and removed the shoring. The picture was taken on registration day as the university began accepting its first students.

the Saudi Arabian embassy in Washington to pick up the check and deposit it in a Washington bank for transfer to our corporate account in Montgomery. The second payment came later that same year. Again, I went to Washington and collected the check personally. I was not about to let the Saudis turn away someone else at the door. I had negotiated the deal and wanted to be absolutely certain there were no more excuses. The moral, if there is one, is that persistence pays off.

What Next?

By 1984, when we completed the university, we knew the Middle East construction market in which we had participated for a decade was winding down. The oil-producing countries of the Middle East had not only completed the modernization of their infrastructure, but they also faced the economic consequences of a worldwide oil glut. The Saudis, in particular, had spent huge amounts of money to modernize their nation, and they did it well. Today, Saudi Arabia's infrastructure is as modern as can be, with six-lane highways and lighted streets, gleaming air-conditioned buildings, state-of-the-art hospitals, modern schools and luxurious hotels.

Meanwhile, at Blount we had been so focused on the Middle East that we had lost our momentum in the construction market in the United States. And, in any event, the U.S. construction market was no longer growing. To get Blount back on track, we had decided on a strategy of acquiring manufacturing companies and applying modern manufacturing techniques to improve their performance.

We needed to do something to change Blount and assure its future. We found the answer in 1985 when we acquired Omark Industries.

CHAPTER EIGHT

Buying Omark, the Heart of Today's Blount International

IF I WERE TO NAME THE 10 MOST IMPORTANT events in Blount's history, I would probably rank the King Saud University project first. But the acquisition of Omark Industries in January 1985 would not be far behind. The Omark acquisition transformed our company and is the foundation of the three divisions — outdoor products, industrial and power equipment, and sporting equipment — that make up Blount International today. Blount would no longer exist if we had not acquired Omark or a company like it. We paid a fancy price, and our bankers cringed at the risk we were taking in doing so. But it turned out to be an excellent deal.

I first heard of Omark in 1983, when Oscar Reak and I went to Japan to study manufacturing techniques in that Asian nation. Japanese manufacturers were beating the pants off of many American companies, and we thought we could learn something by exploring their methods, especially in light of our strategy to acquire manufacturing businesses that were underperforming and improve their results by applying modern manufacturing systems and procedures. We believed we could benefit by using Japanese manufacturing techniques, such as "just-in-time" inventory management, statistical process control and ZIPS.

One of the most interesting people we met in Japan was Dr. Shingo, known as the father of the Toyota manufacturing system. At that time, the Toyota system was supposed to be the key to the Japanese assault on American manufacturing. Dr. Shingo did not

In acquiring Omark, Blount added many quality products, including the saw chain used in chain-saws, opposite, and sporting equipment (left, we manufacture the optical sight on this bow). Omark was founded by an inventor who was chopping firewood and paused for a moment to examine the curious activity in a tree stump. A timber-beetle larva was chewing its way through sound timber, going across and with the wood grain at will. Inspired by what he saw, the inventor came up with a revolutionary new chain, duplicating the larva's alternating C-shaped jaws in steel. This basic design is still widely used today and respresents one of the major advances in the history of timber harvesting.

speak any English. But to every question we asked, he would, through an interpreter, come up with a short and direct answer that made all the sense in the world. According to Dr. Shingo, the secret to Japan's manufacturing success lay in a commonsensical approach to quality and productivity. He described the Japanese concept of *poka-yoke*, roughly equivalent to the English term "idiot-proof." He told us, for instance, how a component being manufactured on a production line would be passed from one work station to the next into a jig which it had to fit precisely. If the component did not fit, it was sent back to the previous station to be corrected. In this way, quality control was integrated into the manufacturing process and did not wait for inspection at the end of the production line.

At the finish of our conversation, I asked Dr. Shingo to name the one or two American companies that, in his view, had been most successful in implementing Japanese manufacturing methods. Without hesitation, he cited Omark Industries of Portland, Oregon. "Who are they?" I wanted to know.

On returning to Montgomery, I turned my attention to learning about Omark. Omark's shares were listed on the New York Stock Exchange, so there was a wealth of information in the public domain, including annual reports and security analyst reviews. I quickly realized that Omark was a well-managed, profitable company that was a good acquisition candidate for Blount if I could convince its owners to sell.

Omark's original name was Oregon Saw Chain Corporation. It was founded in 1947 by an inventor named Joe Cox. While watching a timber-beetle larva, the size of a man's forefinger, chew its way through wood, he came up with the idea for the cutting chain used in chain-saws: the cutting teeth of the chain are like the larva's alternating C-shaped jaws. The modern chain-saw industry grew out of his invention. Omark not only became the dominant supplier of cutting chain to chain-saw manufacturers, but it also diversified into hydraulic loaders, or feller bunchers (we call ours Hydro-Ax), log loaders (our brand is Prentice), sporting goods and other products. By 1983, Omark's sales were approaching $300 million a year. Summarizing the case for Omark as an attractive investment, Moody's Investors Service said, "Acquisitions have broadened product line. Earnings are benefiting from increased demand for chain saws."

The controlling owner of Omark was its vice chairman, John Gray, a native Oregonian. After serving in the army during World War II, rising to the rank of lieutenant colonel, John earned an M.B.A. from Harvard and joined Omark in 1948 as assistant general manager.

This is a Hydro-Ax feller buncher, manufactured by our Industrial and Power Equipment Division, which was part of the Omark acquisition. Feller bunchers are used by forest products companies to harvest trees efficiently. Today, Blount is the leading U.S. manufacturer of feller bunchers.

He moved up the executive ladder rapidly, purchasing the company in 1953, when it was still a fledgling enterprise. He was the brains behind Omark's growth. Although John and I had never met, we were so similar in our interests it was almost spooky. We were both independent-minded entrepreneurs who had been active in the Young Presidents Organization. Moreover, we had both served in the military during World War II, were approximately the same age, collected art and were known for our involvement in civic activities. And just as I was a longtime member of the board of trustees of the University of Alabama and had served as board chairman, John was a longtime member of the board of Reed College in Portland and had served as its chairman. John retired from day-to-day management of Omark in 1983 to develop real estate, but he remained the majority owner and cared deeply about the company and its employees.

I had a good friend in Portland, Bob Warren, a businessman, whom I phoned to ask about John Gray. After describing John, Bob said, "You'll never be able to buy Omark from John Gray. He won't sell. I guarantee it." I decided to find out for myself.

THE WOOING OF OMARK

Before approaching John Gray, we did our homework. A lot of thought went into understanding John and his company's culture and devising a strategy for acquiring Omark.

I felt it was crucial to get to know John and win his confidence before broaching the subject of buying his company. I had my assistant, Shirley Milligan, phone him and say I was chairman of the national Business Committee for the Arts (BCA) and would like to meet him because he was active as an art collector and a supporter of the arts. This was true...as far as it went. I did chair the BCA and did want to discuss art with John. John and I hit it off well at our initial get-together, talking about art and briefly about our companies. I emphasized the many similarities between Omark and Blount. Both were founded after World War II as privately owned businesses. Both had grown rapidly and were respected in their industries. Both were people-oriented, with strong emphasis on professional management. Both were guided by similar philosophies and values. And John and I had many similar personal interests.

At that meeting, I never said anything about acquiring Omark. But I did say, "Maybe we should think about how we could put our companies together." A few days later, I wrote John to the effect that I had enjoyed meeting him.

Our Oregon Cutting Systems Division distributes free seedlings to customers to encourage the renewal of valuable natural resources.

We met again in August 1984. This time, I became more specific about my interest in putting our two companies together if and when the opportunity were to arise. We talked about different ways to unite the companies, and I said I preferred a cash deal. John suggested that our senior people meet to see how they got along. My August meeting with John went well and we agreed to get together again in November.

This was a very busy period for Blount. Even as we were negotiating with John, we were focused on meeting the August 1984 deadline for completing the King Saud University. All in all, it was a remarkable time in the history of our company.

Before the November 1984 meeting, I brought Tom Carruthers of our outside law firm, Bradley Arant, into the negotiations. Together, Tom and I went to New York to get input from Joe Flom. Joe, a senior partner of Skadden, Arps, Slate, Meagher & Flom, is one of the most astute merger and acquisition attorneys in America. After discussing various strategies with Joe, we met with Todd Cunningham at Blount's lead bank, Morgan Guaranty. In seeking to acquire Omark, I wanted to get the best possible advice and did not want to leave anything to chance.

One of John Gray's outstanding qualities is his loyalty to friends and business associates. He wanted to be certain we would treat Omark's employees fairly if we acquired the company. He also wanted assurances that Omark's senior management would have the opportunity to continue to run the company without being nitpicked to death by Blount. To convince him in this regard, we flew our Washington Steel management team to Portland to tell John about their experience under Blount's ownership. They described how they ran their company without undue interference, subject to meeting certain performance standards. I think this visit was pivotal in assuring John that Omark would be in good hands with Blount.

Negotiations picked up speed in the fall. John and I agreed to major terms in November, scheduling a final meeting for January 1985. After the January meeting, I asked Oscar Reak to head a committee with equal membership from Blount and Omark. This committee reviewed all decisions related to the deal and also helped assure that the right relations developed between the top managements of the two companies.

There is no question that the personal relationship that John and I developed made a deal possible. Omark had received a number of acquisition offers. Without our relationship, I believe John never would have sold Omark to Blount.

John wanted a lot of money for Omark. We ended up paying

$280 million cash, but I felt the acquisition was a key to our future and was well worth the price. In fact, Omark turned out to be everything we had expected, and we have been building on it ever since.

Two years after acquiring Omark, we made a massive investment in new machinery to improve product quality. In addition, we expanded its training programs. And in the decade since the acquisition, we have developed a spate of successful new products, such as a diamond chain that cuts through solid concrete as if it were butter, and Woodzig, a power tree-pruner for the consumer market. Moreover, our Omark operations are a global business, now exporting to 130 countries.

At the same time, we have moved forward with Omark's Japanese manufacturing techniques, including just-in-time inventory management. Our success in this regard is highlighted by a number of prestigious awards. In 1991, for instance, the Association for Manufacturing Excellence named our Oregon Cutting Systems Division one of the three best manufacturing companies in America and a model for world-class competitiveness. That sure made me feel good.

Oregon and Omark are two of the premier brand names that came with the Omark acquisition. Sales of Oregon saw chain continue to increase rapidly. We sell to original equipment manufacturers as well as to chain-saw owners for replacement. Quality and reliability are Oregon hallmarks. A recent survey found that Oregon saw chain is preferred four-to-one over the next brand.

Omark was phase one in our plan to expand in manufacturing. Having bought Omark, our goal was to acquire other companies and utilize Omark's manufacturing techniques to improve their competitiveness and earnings. Unfortunately, this plan, which made great sense, had to be put on hold for several years due to financial losses in our domestic construction division. As these losses mounted, Blount's financial position deteriorated and we no longer had the resources to acquire more companies. To the contrary, we were forced to sell our Washington Steel subsidiary to raise funds and stabilize our balance sheet.

Nearly all of my executives opposed the idea of unloading Washington Steel, because it was performing very nicely. I, too, disliked the idea. However, the steel business is capital-intensive, and I felt we would have to invest more than we wanted if we were to grow as a steel manufacturer. In my opinion, given Blount's weak balance sheet, selling Washington Steel was the best option, especially if we could get top dollar. To encourage my executives to share my view and to defuse any potential rancor about the planned sale, at meetings in the office I took to singing:

> You've got to know when to hold 'em,
> You've got to know when to fold 'em.

I am no Kenny Rogers. But I did get my point across — and we all enjoyed a few laughs. Humor and high spirits, when used appropriately, really are effective tools for motivating people and managing a business. The way I see it, there is nothing in the precepts of management that says you have to be somber all the time.

We retained J. P. Morgan & Company, our lead commercial bank, to find a buyer for Washington Steel. It was not long, however, before I lost confidence in the individual at Morgan who was handling the sale. I had several run-ins with him as to how large a price we might expect for the company. Morgan believed Washington Steel would fetch no more than $200 million, while I insisted Morgan had set its sights too low. I kept trying to change this fellow's mind, and there were some tense moments between us.

As it turned out, I was right — although the final days of negotiation were unusual, to say the least. We were down to the wire with the prospective buyer, a German businessman from Chicago, Dietrich Gross, when I headed off to New Orleans to attend the 1988 Republican National Convention as a delegate. Negotiations between Dietrich and a team of Blount executives were taking place at Morgan's offices in New York. Because I was on the convention floor in the Louisiana Superdome (which, incidentally, our company had built 13 years earlier), I could not be reached by phone. So we jerry-rigged a communications network: my wife, Carolyn, stayed at the hotel, receiving calls from the negotiators, and I phoned her periodically for messages. In addition, my assistant, Shirley Milligan, came to New Orleans. One of her tasks was to retrieve and organize faxes. The negotiators in New York would alert her whenever they were sending one, and she would dash downstairs to pull it off the hotel fax machine before anyone else could sneak a look. In this way, we kept the negotiations moving, and we kept them secret.

However, I remained dissatisfied with the price. So I personally took charge of the negotiations, asking Dietrich to fly to New Orleans to meet with me. I had always felt Blount was dealing from a position of strength in the negotiations, because we did not have to sell Washington Steel unless we wanted to. We could simply walk away from the bargaining table if the price was too low. I used that leverage to get a price I thought was fair: $280 million, plus a $5 million note to be paid over several years. Dietrich, rather than being offended, seemed quite satisfied to close the transaction, even though he paid more than he originally had hoped. In fact, he decided a celebration was in order, and he even brought the champagne! So a small group of us partied in our hotel room in New Orleans after signing the agreement, while the negotiators in New York were left to their own devices, which as far as I know did not include Dom Pérignon.

I have always said you can't have the lawyers and bankers settle everything for you. The businesspeople need to get involved. The sale of Washington Steel proved my point.

The sale of Washington Steel gave Blount a large infusion of cash, helping to bail out our construction business. By coincidence, the $280 million we received was the exact same amount as the price we had paid three years earlier to purchase Omark. So in a sense, the two deals offset each other. Washington Steel was and is a fine company. However, if we could own Omark or Washington Steel, one or the other, my druthers would clearly be Omark because of its superior growth potential. So the switch we made in the 1980s — into one manufacturing business and out of another — turned out to be the right decision for Blount. And we did reap a $129 million after-tax profit on Washington Steel, not a bad return on our investment.

When Dietrich Gross, far left in this picture, purchased Washington Steel from Blount, he was so pleased he brought champagne to the contract signing and we celebrated with a toast. Between Dietrich and me is Dan Morris, our in-house attorney. To my left are my wife, Carolyn; my assistant, Shirley Milligan; and Tom Bagley, Dietrich's attorney.

Bill Van Sant, our president, was one of those who did not want to sell Washington Steel. Like the fellow in the TV ads who liked the product so much he bought the company, Bill liked Washington Steel so much that when the opportunity arose later, he bought it.

Bill had joined us as president and chief operating officer in 1987, when Oscar Reak retired. He had been president and chief operating officer of Cessna Aircraft Company, after having spent 25 years with Deere & Company. Two years after joining us, we named Bill our chief executive officer, and I stepped down from that position. Bill was a fine addition to our company and did an excellent job. When he left in 1991 to become chairman and CEO of Lukens, Inc., there was speculation in the media that his performance at Blount had not been up to par. But that was not the case at all. He was not nudged out the door. It was just the opposite. I would have been delighted if he had stayed and, in fact, tried to convince him to do so, but to no avail.

On joining Lukens, one of the first things Bill did was buy Washington Steel for Lukens, paying Dietrich Gross exactly what Dietrich had paid us: $280 million, plus assumption of the $5 million note due Blount. It was dicey whether we would be paid the $5 million until Lukens bought Washington Steel and made payment. Washington Steel continues to be part of Lukens and, according to everything I hear, remains nicely profitable.

MY CHILDREN AND THE COMPANY

It was about this same period of time, in 1989, that my son, Winton, left Blount, Inc. Winton was the only one of my five children to make the company his career. After graduating from the University of the South (Sewanee) and the Wharton Business School, he joined our construction division and worked his way up to become the division's president. He has great energy and ambition, and he did an outstanding job. As my oldest son, he expected, quite understandably, that he would one day succeed me as CEO. But when Oscar Reak retired and I was looking for a new president, I wanted someone with a manufacturing background and recruited Bill Van Sant. I told Winton that he and Bill were in competition for the CEO's job.

Two years later, when I made my choice, because Winton was construction-oriented and the direction of the company was toward manufacturing, I selected Bill. I found it emotionally wrenching to bypass my son, but I believed Bill was the right person to head the company at that time. Although I encouraged Winton to stay with Blount, he felt betrayed and left. That happens in many companies: you select one person and the other leaves. Of course, it is a different matter altogether when the one who leaves is your own son. My children, grandchildren and great-grandchildren are very important to me. I love them deeply, and it was unsettling to be at odds with Winton. Happily, this episode is now behind us. Time has healed the wounds, I hope, and Winton and I are once again on friendly terms.

Winton is smart and resilient. After leaving Blount, he went into business for himself and has been very successful. In fact, all four of my sons are successful entrepreneurs. Winton owns a string of businesses, from car dealerships to a plastics company, and in 1994 was the Republican candidate for governor of Alabama. Tom is an Atlanta architect who did a magnificent job in designing the Carolyn Blount Theatre at our Alabama Shakespeare Festival in Montgomery. Writing in the *Washington Post*, drama critic Richard Coe described the facility as "the most beautiful...theater building I've seen on five continents." Sam worked at Blount early in his career and now owns the nation's largest wrought-iron furniture business, based in Birmingham and Atlanta. He was recently named "vendor of the year" by Wal-Mart, a tremendous recognition of his success. He also serves on the board of Discovery 2000, a science museum planned for Birmingham. And Joe, my youngest son, owns a very successful home decorating/distribution business, including furniture, lighting and accessories; based in Atlanta, it is expanding across the United States. My daughter, Kay, who lives in Birmingham, is a very bright, talented and energetic woman who is raising a family and is very active in the community. She is co-chair of the Birmingham Festival of the Arts, honoring the country of Korea, its culture and its art. This is a very challenging assignment that will last about 18 months. Her co-chair is the immediate past president of the University of Alabama medical complex in Birmingham. By all accounts, Kay is doing an outstanding job and is a wonderful asset to Birmingham and Alabama. She has also co-chaired the Birmingham Museum Ball. Her three children, my grandchildren, are all developing nicely. All of my children have done well and I am proud of them.

Long ago, I made each of my children financially well off by giving them stock in Blount. Together as a family, we control a majority of the company's voting shares. Until very recently, these shares were owned through a family holding company, HBC, Inc. We wanted to call the company BHC, for Blount Holding Company, but someone else was already using that name, so we rearranged the letters and came up with HBC. My children owned the common stock of

HBC and I owned the preferred stock, which had all the votes. In this way, I retained control of Blount, while my children had major equity ownership. In late 1995, in a transaction approved by Blount shareholders, we combined Blount with HBC. The name of the holding company is now Blount International, Inc.; Blount, Inc., became a wholly owned subsidiary of the holding company. Our public shareholders, as well as my children and I, continue to own stock, but in Blount International, Inc., rather than in Blount, Inc.

One of the ironies of entrepreneurship is that you work hard to build a business and create security for yourself and your children, yet success and wealth can create tensions that tear families apart. There have been a number of highly publicized examples of wealthy families succumbing to this pernicious phenomenon. I was determined not to let it happen to the Blounts.

Beginning in 1982, with the help of my advisers Bob Bleke and Tom Carruthers, we held a series of family meetings to keep my children up to date on the business and bring any disputes out into the open so they could be discussed and, hopefully, resolved. Were my children satisfied with Blount's financial performance? What, if anything, did they expect from the company beyond their role as shareholders? Did they expect their own children to work for the company? These were just a few of the types of questions that were discussed.

It was fascinating to take part in these meetings and see the different attitudes within the family. Anybody who has raised children knows they have minds of their own. My children do, and I love them for it. Raising children to be independent thinkers is part of the fun of parenthood. It is also one of the ironies: you want your children to think for themselves, but it's hard to understand why they keep disagreeing with you. At one meeting, Bob Bleke divided us into groups based on how we felt about a particular question (I forget what it was). My son, Sam, and I ended up together in one corner of the room because we agreed. Others were in other groups around the room, highlighting the differences among us. We all looked at each other, astonished at who was aligned with whom. We had never before seen our differences so clearly. It isn't always pleasant to discuss conflicts within a family. But sweeping them under the rug is even more unpleasant in the long run. Bob Bleke says that meetings of this sort are unusual in family-controlled enterprises. Based on my experience, I would recommend them to any family that owns a business. They are a valuable device to get everybody singing from the same hymnbook, even if they don't always sing in perfect harmony.

After Winton left Blount, with the tensions surrounding that event, we discontinued the meetings for a period. They were resumed in 1992, but at Bob Bleke's suggestion, I no longer take part. In many of the meetings, Blount management attends to answer questions, and my children are able to discuss their concerns and reach their own conclusions without the old man looking over their shoulders

MY EXTENDED FAMILY

Carolyn has two children who are very much a part of our family. Her daughter, Stuart, is married to George King and is very active in the Humane Society. Stuart loves animals, especially cats and dogs. She has a huge Rottweiler named Otto. Otto is well trained and she has excellent control of him, but he still scares me.

Carolyn's son, Ed, is a highly respected doctor at UAB in Birmingham, as is his lovely wife, Pam. They have two wonderful children, Stuart Ann, ten years old, and Duncan, seven. Stuart Ann is smart, and is talented in ballet and skiing. Duncan is also very bright and draws and paints, and we have a special way of talking to each other that nobody else understands.

Most of my children and grandchildren call me Red. When Stuart Ann was 3½ years old she told her father, "When I grow up I'm going to have three children — two girls and a boy — and I'm going to call the boy Red." Her father asked, "Is that because he will have red hair?" She replied, "No, he'll have white hair." I knew then she was talking about me.

Former PepsiCo Chairman Don Kendall is today my closest friend. We hunt, ski or bicycle together, or just tell stories and have a great time. In February 1996, to celebrate my 75th birthday, some of my friends threw a gala benefit, "Paint the Town Red," for the Alabama Shakespeare Festival. Don showed up and gave $100,000 worth of PepsiCo stock to the Festival. Now that's the kind of friend everybody should have!

CHAPTER NINE

Man Does Not Live by Bread Alone

IT WAS DURING MY YEARS IN GOVERNMENT SERvice and when I first returned to Blount that I began to develop an interest in the arts. I jumped right in, and the arts soon became one of the passions of my life, remaining so today. In fact, one magazine recently called Carolyn and me "patrons with a flair." I'm not exactly sure what "with a flair" means, but we do have great fun supporting theater groups, museums, ballet companies, orchestras and other arts organizations, including the Alabama Shakespeare Festival right here in Montgomery and the Bolshoi International Ballet in Vail.

Arts sponsorship is also part of Blount International's corporate culture. It is one of the values that makes our company special. Blount's association with the arts has been a big plus in recruitment, has surprised and delighted our customers, and has shown that we care about people. Inspired in some cases by our corporate leadership, many of our employees have personally become involved, lending their support to cultural organizations as volunteers or through financial contributions. It is one of the thrills of my life to see so many of our employees take an active role in the community — in cultural organizations, religious groups, community service projects and myriad other worthy causes. Volunteerism is one of the vital strengths of American society, and I cannot say enough about the great job the people of Blount do in this regard.

Opposite , *Summer Twilight* by Stuart Davis. We acquired this painting for the Blount Corporate Collection and later donated it, along with other major paintings, to the Montgomery Museum of Fine Arts. Left, detail from *Flower Market, Cuernavaca,* by James Asher. Carolyn and I met Jim Asher on our first trip to Santa Fe, and I bought this picture for the Blount Corporate Collection. Jim is one of the finest artists of our time working in watercolor. His works are so detailed they look like photographs, which is very difficult to accomplish in watercolor.

After making our major donation of paintings to the Montgomery Museum of Fine Arts, we began acquiring works by younger artists to replenish our corporate collection. *The Bathers,* by John Asaro, was one of the first in this new round of acquisitions.

My love affair with the arts began rather unexpectedly, some 25 years ago, when I was postmaster general of the United States. While visiting a post office in Detroit, I came upon a room full of paintings and was told it was the annual art exhibit of employees. Previously, I had a general interest in art, but this show struck a responsive chord unlike any exhibition I had seen before. I was impressed not only by the quality of the paintings, but also by their sincere expression of personal emotion. I thought about the Post Office Department's 750,000 employees, most of them in dead-end jobs at that time. Many of the employees were African-Americans, and a great number of the paintings portrayed the black experience. Sparked by this show, I decided the Post Office should organize a national exhibition of employees' paintings. That decision led to the annual National Postal Art Show, which gives visibility to the talents of postal employees nationwide and helps lift their spirits.

When I returned to Blount in 1973, many corporations were gearing up to celebrate the 1976 American bicentennial. There was no national theme — just do your own thing. I wanted Blount to celebrate the bicentennial in a way that was unique and meaningful. Having seen how art could engage and motivate people in the Postal Service, I decided to assemble a collection of American paintings that could be displayed not only in Blount's offices, but could also be made available for viewing by the public. I had no particular ideas about which artists' work to include. I just wanted to bring together a collection of outstanding paintings from across the 200-year sweep of our nation's history.

I had read in *Time* and *Newsweek* about Larry Fleischman, one of the premier dealers in American art. Larry owned Kennedy Galleries, then located on East 76th Street in New York. One afternoon, I dropped by unannounced and spent two-and-a-half hours with him, looking at pictures. To say I was naive about prices is an understatement. I told Larry I wanted to buy American paintings at a top price of $500 each. He did not say a word about my budget. Instead, he let the prices speak for themselves. I didn't buy anything that day, but I did make a mental note to add some zeros to my $500 limit.

That was the first of many visits with Larry, who, with his exuberant personality and wide-ranging personal interests, would make a perfect subject for one of those *Reader's Digest* memorable character articles. Short and stocky, with wavy black hair, Larry has been described by his wife, Barbara, as being "an amalgam of characteristics and contradictions, a shrewd, tough and canny man whose exterior masks his sensitive, sentimental and intuitive side." I would add such words as outspoken, energetic, fun-loving and unpretentious.

Larry and I became buddies. I like being with him because he is very smart, enjoys having a good time and is never at a loss for words. We both also happen to love ice cream and, on our trips to Rome (I'll get to that shortly), we always make a special point of having some at the famous Giolitti ice cream shop near Piazza Colonna.

In my early visits to Larry's gallery, I began to see what made one painter's work more interesting than another's, and I started to explore my personal taste. I do not consider myself an art expert. However, I do know what I like and don't like — and I bought paintings based on my preferences, relying on Larry to ensure authenticity and quality.

One of my first acquisitions was Stuart Davis's *Summer Twilight*, painted in 1931, for which I paid about $100,000. So much for $500 pictures! *Summer Twilight* is Davis at his best: juxtapositions of abstract forms and realistic images that convey liveliness and rhythm. Another early acquisition was Edward Hopper's quiet but intense *New York Office*, painted in 1962.

New York Office, by Edward Hopper, is one of the most important paintings ever owned by Blount. It, too, was included in our gift to the Montgomery Museum of Fine Arts. The museum has said of this work, "Hopper intends no overt narrative but suggests the cold detachment of urban life with its empty alleys, blank windows and humans who are inaccessible behind curtain walls of glass."

We selected Gary Price's bronze sculpture, *Ascent*, above, for the Blount Corporate Collection because of the strong statement it makes about challenge and teamwork. Neither Indian would make it to the top of the cliff without the other. At Blount, it takes all of us pulling together as a team to be successful. We bought *The Steelworker*, by N. C. Wyeth, right, when we owned a steel company. It is one of the finest works in our corporate collection today.

It was a long, challenging and exhilarating process to assemble a collection of first-rate American paintings that appealed to my taste. I looked at many, many paintings for every one I bought. The collection eventually included nearly 100 works, dating from the 1770s through the mid-twentieth century, by such artists as John Singleton Copley, Frederic Church, Winslow Homer, Mary Cassatt, John Singer Sargent, Marsden Hartley, Charles Burchfield, Georgia O'Keeffe, Jack Levine and Andrew Wyeth, among many others.

In 1988, our company gave 42 of the best paintings, valued at some $15 million, to the Montgomery Museum of Fine Arts. The museum has said the Blount Collection of American Art, as these paintings are called, is the single most important gift it has ever received. When I first started collecting, many people at Blount thought I was nuts to keep heading off to New York to buy expensive pictures. But they came to love the paintings (great art grows on you), and they were even more befuddled when I gave so many of them to the museum. They said, "Why is he giving away *our* paintings?"

Sometimes I am asked to name my favorite work in the collection. But that is like being asked to name my favorite child. I love them all — my children and my paintings.

Larry Fleischman quickly drew me into his web of art-world public service activities. He decided I am someone who likes to get involved — and, of course, he was right!

In 1971, Larry had been asked by Pope Paul VI to help obtain fine examples of twentieth-century American art for the Vatican Museum. Larry invited me to join this effort by becoming a member of the Friends of American Art in Religion, on which I continue to serve today. The committee was headed by Terence Cardinal Cooke of the Archdiocese of New York. Its secretary was an astute, affable priest, Monsignor Eugene Clark, also from New York. Larry and I received a lot of good-natured kidding about our affiliation with the Vatican. Several people, mostly Catholics, wanted to know what a New York Jew and a South Alabama Baptist were doing hanging out with a crowd like that. We have had a great time over the years.

It was through the committee that I came to know Pope Paul VI, one of the most extraordinary individuals I have met in my lifetime. Pope Paul was urbane and gracious and, despite the tradition and formality of his office, had a wonderful ability to put people at ease. In 1976, I had the opportunity to chair a three-day seminar, "The Influence of Spiritual Inspiration on American Art," in Rome. The seminar was attended by 300 artists, collectors and religious leaders from around the world and was simultaneously translated into three languages. The pope was not scheduled to participate. However, he was a great believer in the power of art to communicate the divine and he clearly thought the conference was important. So it was not a total surprise when, in the middle of one session, we were suddenly informed that the pope was on his way by helicopter to join us and deliver a brief address. The room was immediately emptied while security people checked for bombs, after which we filed back in and took our seats with eager anticipation. Moments later, the pope walked through the door in his white vestments and headed toward the dais, where I was standing. As he approached, I asked His Holiness to take a seat while I introduced him. I was chairman of the meeting and had been introducing all the scholars and thought it only natural to welcome the pope. His Holiness seemed slightly taken aback, and it was only later that I learned that, according to Vatican protocol, the pope is never introduced. Being who he is, he simply gets up and talks. Larry still refers to me as the only person in the world who ever had the privilege, or the audacity, to introduce Pope Paul VI.

As I became more involved in the arts, I got to know the CEOs of other U.S. companies that were also buying paintings. It dawned on me that corporations were becoming the modern-day Medicis supporting the arts, and I thought it would be great to put together a show of premier American works from corporate collections. We came up with the title "Art, Inc." It was a blockbuster exhibition of works from the collections of PepsiCo, Westinghouse, General Electric, Chase Manhattan Bank, Blount and many others. We opened it in 1979 in the Montgomery Museum of Fine Arts, putting our then-little museum on the map. The exhibition highlighted the growth of corporate support of the arts. In addition, by taking the show to regional museums, we demonstrated there is an audience for art all over the country, not just in the largest cities. I have always believed that collecting and viewing art is not an elitist activity — that there is a vast audience of Americans who enjoy art even if they don't hold advanced degrees in the history of painting. The great success of the regional tour of Art, Inc., proved that very point. After its tour of regional museums, the federal government extended the show to eight foreign countries.

The night of the opening in Montgomery, I had a gala party at my home. Several of us, including Larry Fleischman and Gene Clark (of the Friends of American Art in Religion), were chatting when someone asked, "What are you going to do for an encore, Red?" Without giving it much thought, I replied, "We ought to get the Vatican to let us borrow some of its treasures and bring them to the United States." I said a touring exhibition of Vatican masterpieces would draw huge audiences and we could open it right here in

The Montgomery Museum of Fine Arts building, completed in 1988, is one of the most magnificent museum facilities of its size in the world. With our first-class museum, our Alabama Shakespeare Festival and other cultural organizations and activities, Montgomery is establishing itself as a cultural center of the South.

Montgomery. Well, it was a great idea. And it turned out to be a great exhibition. But it only toured the big cities; Montgomery never did get included on the itinerary.

Because of our connection with the Vatican, Larry Fleischman and I were both involved in the negotiations to arrange the exhibition. The negotiating sessions, translated simultaneously into three languages, were held in a large, ornate room at the Vatican, lighted only by a big chandelier. During an especially difficult session when the negotiations seemed about to get stuck, the lights suddenly went out. Moments later, just as unexpectedly, they came back on. I looked over to Carolyn, who was seated by the wall observing the talks, and she pointed to the light switch behind her and mouthed to me that she had hit it by mistake. However, her miscue did serve a purpose:

Negotiations for the first-ever United States touring exhibition of masterpieces from the Vatican collection were conducted over an extended period at Vatican City. I'm at the far left in this negotiating session. Other participants include art dealer Larry Fleischman, standing; Baron Heinrich Thyssen-Bornemisza, a prominent European art collector, seated to Larry's left; Monsignor Eugene Clark of the Friends of American Art in Religion, directly beneath the painting, with his hand to his mouth; and Walter Persegati, chief administrator of the Vatican Museum, lower right, with the back of his head to the camera. Below, I received this medal from Pope John Paul II for community service, including my role in bringing the Vatican exhibition to the United States.

the brief blackout broke the tensions and enabled us to resume our negotiations in a more relaxed spirit. Walter Persegati, chief administrator of the Vatican Museum, said, "Divine intervention." To which I replied, "No, Walter, my wife's intervention."

This first-ever touring exhibition of Vatican art to the United States took place in 1983. I was awarded two papal medals for my role in helping make it possible. Perhaps Carolyn should have received one, too.

182

Left to right, Baron Thyssen-Bornemisza, Larry
Fleischman, Carolyn and I were in high spirits after
negotiations for the American tour of Vatican
art had been successfully concluded.

Carolyn and I had the privilege of being invited
by Pope John Paul II to the rededication of the
Sistine Chapel in 1994. Only about 20 of us were
present as *The Last Judgment*, newly restored, was
fully lighted. It was a breathtaking
experience.

WHY I SUPPORT FEDERAL FUNDING OF THE ARTS

Today, I remain as active as ever in the arts, serving on the boards of such organizations as the Alabama Shakespeare Festival in Montgomery; the National Actors Theatre in New York; the Royal Shakespeare Theatre in Stratford-on-Avon, England; the Folger Shakespeare Library; the Business Committee for the Arts, Inc.; and the American Council for the Arts.

Moreover, in these times when public funding of the arts is under attack from nay-sayers in and out of government, I have become more outspoken than ever in my views about the indispensable role of the arts in our society.

In March 1995, I was honored to give the annual Nancy Hanks Lecture on Arts and Public Policy, sponsored by the American Council for the Arts, at the Kennedy Center in Washington. This occasion was especially meaningful for me, because I knew Nancy Hanks, who chaired the National Endowment for the Arts in the Nixon administration. President Nixon supported government funding of the arts, and through Nancy's leadership, the National Endowment experienced unprecedented growth during the Nixon years.

In my speech, I noted that federal funding of the arts is "one of the few federal programs that has both bipartisan support and the overwhelming majority approval of the American people." I also said, "The issue under debate, purely and simply, should be, Do the arts contribute to the public commonweal? Is art an inevitable component of the good society? If some believe it is not, let them say so. And let them offer us examples of nations that have achieved greatness while turning their backs on art."

Publicly funded programs make art democratic. To suggest that the arts should rely solely for their health on private funding is, in my opinion, a form of snobbery. It implies that those without means are incapable of producing art or of appreciating it.

The Alabama Shakespeare Festival is a beneficiary of the National Endowment for the Arts. We are grateful for that support, but we would not perish without it. Others, however, would.

The Montgomery Symphony Association awarded me a Silver Baton for my support of music performance and education organizations. As the orchestra started to play, I put my newly awarded baton to use by conducting a few measures.

SILVER BATON AWARD
For Support of Symphonic Music Education and Performance

Winton M. Blount, Chairman and Chief Executive Officer of Blount, Inc., has been chosen to receive this first Silver Baton Award for his achievements and contributions in furthering the cause of symphonic music in the Montgomery area: his early support of the Montgomery Symphony Orchestra, his initial and continuing support of the Young Artists' Competition and performance with the orchestra, youth music scholarships and youth symphony; as well as his generous support of music education and enrichment in the community through the underwriting of classical music training at the Carver Creative and Performing Arts Center; and for his patronage and encouragement of classical music performances at the Alabama Shakespeare Festival and The Carolyn Blount Theatre, Jasmine Hill Amphitheatre, Jubilee Pops concerts at Riverfront Park, Brown Bag concerts on Court Square, the Chamber Music Organization and other musical associations, educational institutions and performing arts groups which are helping to enhance through symphonic music the quality of life for people in south central Alabama and the nation.

Presented by the
Montgomery Symphony Association
September 29, 1986

MONTGOMERY: EMERGING CENTER OF THE ARTS

One of my goals has been to work with others in making Montgomery a cultural center of the South, a place people want to visit and one where the quality of life for our citizens is second to none. I think our community has come a long way toward accomplishing that objective, not only with our year-round Alabama Shakespeare Festival but also with our splendid Montgomery Museum of Fine Arts.

It is always a pleasure to watch the eager faces of people as they enter the Shakespeare Festival or the Montgomery Museum. But it is astonishing to see their faces as they come out. They are, in their shared experience, new people, aware of things they only dreamed before, or did not dream at all. Art has done its job.

CHAPTER TEN

A Shakespeare Theater
in Our Backyard...
It's a Mighty Big Backyard

OVER THE YEARS, I HAD ASSEMBLED 250 ACRES of beautiful rolling land around my home with the idea of using it for some higher purpose. I thought about a public garden and other possibilities, but the right idea never seemed to come along... until one morning in 1982, a year after Carolyn and I were married.

My appointment calendar that morning included a meeting with representatives of the Alabama Shakespeare Festival. ASF was a nationally acclaimed theater company that performed six weeks each summer in a high school auditorium in Anniston, about 100 miles northeast of Montgomery. Although I had never seen any of its plays, I knew about ASF through Carolyn, who had been attending its performances each summer since its founding a decade earlier. ASF had a reputation for staging first-class productions of works by Shakespeare and other playwrights on a shoestring budget. Like many other nonprofit theater groups, it struggled to make ends meet. In fact, years earlier, when Carolyn gave ASF a $50 donation, the founders were so thrilled they invited her to join the ASF board of directors.

At breakfast that morning, I said to Carolyn, "I'm looking at my schedule today and I see I have an appointment with that theater company in Anniston. Aren't you on that board?" She said, "Yes." I said, "Do you want to tell me what it's about?" She said, "No." I assumed they were going to ask for money.

Opposite, I posed in front of the 250-acre empty field by our home prior to groundbreaking for the Carolyn Blount Theatre. Contrast this picture with the photograph on page 199 of the completed theater, man-made lake and landscaped grounds. Left, someone from Montgomery — I never found out who — saw this carved bust of Shakespeare in an antique shop in Maine and told the owner that a fellow in Alabama named Red Blount might want to buy it. The antique dealer sent me photographs, and I acquired it for the Patrons Room of the Carolyn Blount Theatre.

When I arrived at my office and found that all of ASF's big guns had come to the meeting, I *knew* they were going to ask for money. The delegation was led by Martin Platt, the founder and artistic director, and included Josie Ayers, the executive producer, as well as Bill Davis, a board member and businessman from Anniston, and Charlie Doster, an Anniston attorney. They immediately got to the point: ASF was in desperate financial condition. They were coming to me as a last resort, asking for $80,000 to bail them out. Absent such a donation, they planned to file for bankruptcy. Before giving an answer, I had my financial people look over ASF's books, which produced an interesting surprise for all of us: by their estimate, ASF needed $300,000, not $80,000, to stave off bankruptcy.

It was at about that point that an idea popped into my head: I thought about the land behind my home, and I felt the Alabama Shakespeare Festival was too good for our state to lose. I also realized that ASF needed to be in a larger community in a modern facility where it could perform year-round to survive and grow. I then asked our legal people to examine the condition of ASF, and I phoned Carolyn and said, "This is getting interesting. Why don't you come over?"

At the end of the day, with all the information from our financial and legal people in hand, I asked the group from Anniston to come into my office to review the situation with Carolyn and me. I said, "You have two problems. One, you are bankrupt and can't open your doors. And two, you cannot continue to run a Shakespeare theater with the high standard of excellence you want in a six-week season with a total attendance of 20,000 annually." I then said that if ASF would move to Montgomery, Carolyn and I would build a theater for its year-round use and would also bail the group out of its debts. As I recall, Martin Platt accepted the offer even before he could jump out of his seat.

We continued our discussion and the entire group then headed off to Wynfield, our home, about two miles from the office, to look at the 250 acres. Everybody was pleased with the site, and the next day ASF announced it had accepted my offer to build it a theater on a 250-acre site in Montgomery.

ASF was a matter of civic pride for the people of Anniston, a community of 30,000. Understandably, many of them were disappointed when ASF announced it would be leaving for Montgomery. However, Josie Ayers' husband, Brandy Ayers, who owned the Anniston newspaper and, like Josie, had been active in ASF since its beginning, put the matter in perspective with the headline, "Better Red Than Dead."

In my mind, I was thinking of a modest-sized theater that might cost $4 million to build, or $5 million at most. Boy, was I in for a surprise.

VISITING REGIONAL THEATERS

Following our initial meeting, which took place in May 1982, a series of events occurred in quick order.

In June, I called my son, Tom, an architect in Atlanta, and asked him to design the theater.

Two months after that, in August 1982, our entire team — including Tom Blount, Martin Platt, Carolyn and myself — took two swings around North America to visit regional theater companies. They included the Stratford, Ontario, Shakespearean Festival; the Shaw Festival in Niagara-on-the-Lake, Ontario; the Guthrie Theatre in Minneapolis; the Ashland, Oregon, Shakespeare Festival; and San Diego's Old Globe Theater; among others. At each stop, we looked at the physical layout and inquired about the challenges of running a regional theater — where the revenues came from, what the expenses were, production requirements and so on.

Visiting the Stratford, Ontario, Shakespearean Festival as part of our tour of regional theaters, our group included, left to right: Carol Ballard, who was Blount's coordinator of cultural affairs; Josie Ayers, executive producer of ASF; Jan Howard, a friend of Carolyn's who attended ASF performances with her and is a member of the ASF board; architect Tom Blount; Martin Platt, ASF's founder and artistic director; and me.

Many of the leading theaters, we discovered, encompassed two facilities: a main theater for large productions and a smaller one for experimental plays and those with a limited audience. If ASF was to rank among the best, it would need to have the same. My $4 million estimate was already beginning to move up.

We also learned that 50 percent to 80 percent of a nonprofit theater company's revenue typically comes from ticket sales and the remainder from government funding and private contributions. Given the high costs of staging live drama, it is virtually impossible for a nonprofit company to be self-supporting from ticket sales alone. One of the theaters that intrigued me most, and which no longer exists today, was the American Shakespeare Festival Theater and Academy in Stratford, Connecticut. It had been built by a man who not only donated the building but funded its operations. When he died, the funding stopped, and there was no longer a support system to keep the theater going. The theater was closed, was subsequently reopened by the State of Connecticut, and was closed again, this time permanently because it could not compete with the Broadway theaters in nearby New York.

I took the lessons of Stratford, Connecticut, to heart. One of the morals was the need to develop a broad base of financial support. Building a Shakespeare theater may sound very romantic — and it is. But there are also harsh business realities. I felt it was imperative to find out as soon as possible whether the public and private sectors in Alabama were willing to support a theater.

I met with Jim Martin, the president of Auburn University, and then with Tom Bartlett, chancellor of the University of Alabama, and told them of the planned theater, enlisting them as allies. They recognized immediately that a nonprofit theater would be a tremendous resource for their institutions. Indeed, 19 Alabama universities and colleges later formed a consortium to develop academic programs in association with ASF. Among those programs, the University of Alabama now utilizes ASF as a major facility for educating master's degree candidates in acting, stage management and theater management.

Jim and Tom went with me to see Governor George Wallace. I told the governor that Carolyn and I planned to build a theater at our expense and donate it to the people of Alabama. I also discussed the information we had gathered from nonprofit theaters across North America, noting it might be appropriate for the state legislature, speaking for the people of Alabama, to help subsidize ASF's operating costs in its new facility. ASF's projected annual operating budget was about $6 million. We expected to generate about half that amount from ticket sales and other sources, but we needed to raise the balance from state and local government and from contributions by corporations, foundations and individuals.

The governor agreed to support an annual appropriation of $750,000. With that endorsement, I went to see the leaders of the Alabama House of Representatives and Senate. They, too, gave their support, and the legislature has been generous in funding ASF ever since. By the early 1990s, our state funding had moved up to $950,000 a year. However, the state economy then went into a tailspin, whereupon ASF's funding was completely wiped off the books in the first draft of the state budget. All of us associated with ASF fought like blazes, and ASF ended up receiving an appropriation of $700,000. We understood the realities of the state's budgetary pressures and were grateful for the $700,000. Since then, our state funding has moved back up to $900,000, which meets about 15 percent of ASF's operating expenses.

I also went to see Emory Folmar, whom I admire greatly. He has been mayor of Montgomery since the late 1970s and has encouraged all the good causes in the city and combatted what is bad. He put the city behind our efforts to set up a support system to maintain the grounds, which relieved us of substantial costs. In addition, the city made a financial commitment to ASF and continues to do so today. The county commission joined in with financial support for the theater.

I then began to go around the state talking with the CEO's of major corporations and banks. Again, I was successful. Today, corporations and foundations throughout the Southeast, including such companies as Delta Air Lines, Coca-Cola, Union Camp Corporation, all the major banks and, of course, Blount International, support ASF.

We also receive support from hundreds of individual contributors and a number of foundations, and also get some support from the National Endowment for the Arts.

All of this effort may sound like a lot of work, but that's what it takes to build a consensus and raise funds for an organization like ASF. To open governance to all segments of the community, ASF has a 61-member board of directors that includes elected officials, community leaders, educators, business people and many others. If we are to receive public funding, we must be inclusive in our governance practices. Doing so is part of our strategy of building the community's sense of ownership of ASF.

Because we have such a strong, broadly based support system, we have not encountered the financial problems that have beset so many other nonprofit theater companies. To make sure ASF can survive long-term and continue to stage quality productions, regardless of fluctuations in funding, we are in the midst of a $15 million endowment campaign called The Festival Forever. To the degree possible, we want to insulate ASF's creative decisions from financial considerations.

TOM BLOUNT HITS A HOME RUN: A CLASSICAL DESIGN

When we got back from our visits to the regional theaters, Tom Blount returned to Atlanta and began working with his partner, Perry Pittman, on some architectural concepts. Tom felt the theater should be compatible with the Georgian architecture of Carolyn's and my home, so he designed it in a style reminiscent of the work of Renaissance architect Andrea Palladio. The Palladian style combines classical elements, such as columns and arches, with the use of

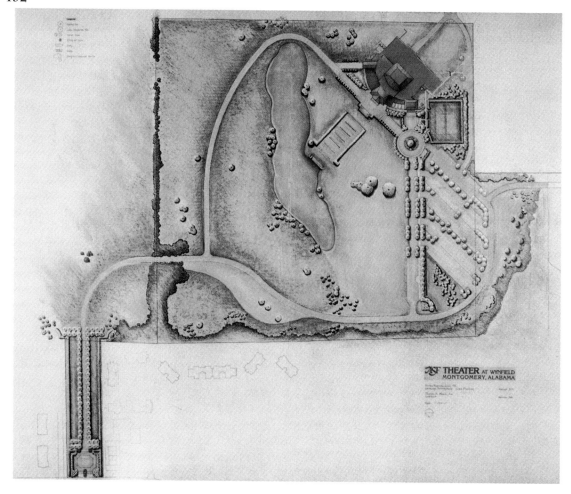

THEATER AT WYNFIELD
MONTGOMERY, ALABAMA

This is one of Tom Blount's early sketches for the proposed siting of the theater. Carolyn and I were delighted with his initial drawings for the architecture and siting, which he showed us in 1982.

brick or other everyday construction materials. The most famous Palladio-inspired building in America is Thomas Jefferson's Monticello. When Tom Blount came to Montgomery with a series of sketches and pinned them on a wall, Carolyn and I were just stunned by their beauty. Those drawings quickly evolved into the theater as it is today. There was very little fuss about the architecture. We were happy from the start.

I still hadn't told Carolyn I was going to name the theater for her. I was saving that as a surprise.

Meanwhile, I retained Russell Page, the renowned British landscape architect, to design the grounds. Russell was designing the gardens at PepsiCo's corporate headquarters in Purchase, New York, and was recommended to me by my friend, PepsiCo chairman Don Kendall. Russell was in his late 70s. When I invited him to Montgomery, he initially turned me down, saying he wasn't taking on any more assignments. But I finally convinced him to work with us, and he made his first trip to Montgomery in July 1983. I didn't want Russell to exhaust himself by traipsing about the field in the summer heat, so I found a golf cart with a fringe on top for his use. Russell spent three days in Montgomery on his first visit, staying at our home. He rose early each morning and was out working while everyone else was still asleep. But he never did ride in that golf cart. Instead, he used it as a motorized wheelbarrow, filling it with stakes which he stuck in the ground to lay out his design. One of his many contributions was to site the theater atop a hill, facing a grove of trees, so that the first thing people see when they come through that grove is the theater directly in front of them. It's a spectacular sight.

In his drawings, Tom had included a sketch of a lake by the theater. Tom tends to talk slowly, dragging out his words. He said to Russell, "I'm thinking of this lake going right along here. What do you think?" With his snappy British wit, Russell replied, "It looks like a dried-up centipede to me." Tom just fell out laughing and said,

We met Russell Page, left, one of the world's preeminent landscape architects, through my good friend Don Kendall of PepsiCo. Carolyn and I became very fond of Russell, who was so wonderfully bright and witty. Russell designed the landscaping for the Carolyn Blount Theatre but, sadly, did not live to see the completion of his work.

"What do you want it to be?" Russell said, "I want it much bigger. And I want to put it where it reflects the theater." And that is exactly what he did.

To add an Elizabethan touch to the lake, we decided to populate it with a flock of black and white swans. John Lesenger, our gardener at Wynfield, called the Royal Shakespeare Theatre in Stratford, England, to find out where they got their swans. We were flabbergasted to learn they bought them from a breeder right outside Montgomery. We should have looked in the yellow pages.

Russell Page never lived to see his work completed. He died in December 1984, a year before the theater opened. The landscaping for the theater and the surrounding cultural park was one of the last major projects of this celebrated landscape architect.

An "Unlimited" Budget — and We Exceeded It!

I sometimes say I gave my son an unlimited budget and he exceeded it. However, as Tom makes clear, the price kept going up for a number of reasons unrelated to his design. For one, the theater consultants we hired kept adding features, such as additional technical capabilities and more rehearsal, costume-making and storage space. No matter how much we added, they wanted even more. There were also many lovely design touches which escalated the cost. Examples include the massive oak doors and the bronze sculpture of Puck, one of Shakespeare's most beloved characters, created in Italy by Elizabeth MacQueen, an Alabama native. The building itself is faced with one million "Shakespeare Blend" bricks, developed specially for us by Jenkins Brick Company of Montgomery.

Shakespeare exerts his presence in the Patrons Room of the theater. I have an indirect connection to the Bard. My ancestor, Edward Blount, was a London printer who held the original publishing rights to *Antony and Cleopatra*, *Pericles* and other Shakespeare plays.

We went first class all the way, which was fine up to a point. However, in June 1983, two months before groundbreaking, Tom came to me and said the project had gotten out of hand. The theater, he believed, had become 40 percent too big and far too expensive. I said, "Okay, cut 40 percent." He did so, reworking all his designs in just a week, a herculean task. Even with those cuts, the theater ended up costing $22 million, which has been described as the largest single gift ever made to an American theater company. I shouldn't have been surprised because 15 years earlier, when I built my house, I thought it would cost one-third of what it did.

I have no regrets. The Carolyn Blount Theatre, housing the 750-seat Festival Stage and the 225-seat Octagon, is truly one of the most beautiful facilities of its kind in the world. It is worth every penny I paid.

Groundbreaking took place on August 10, 1983. We put up a big tent and invited friends of ASF, as well as government officials and community leaders, to the ceremony. One of the speakers was Governor Wallace. I do not recall his exact words, but they were something to the effect, "I like the way Red gets a job done. He does great things and pays for them himself."

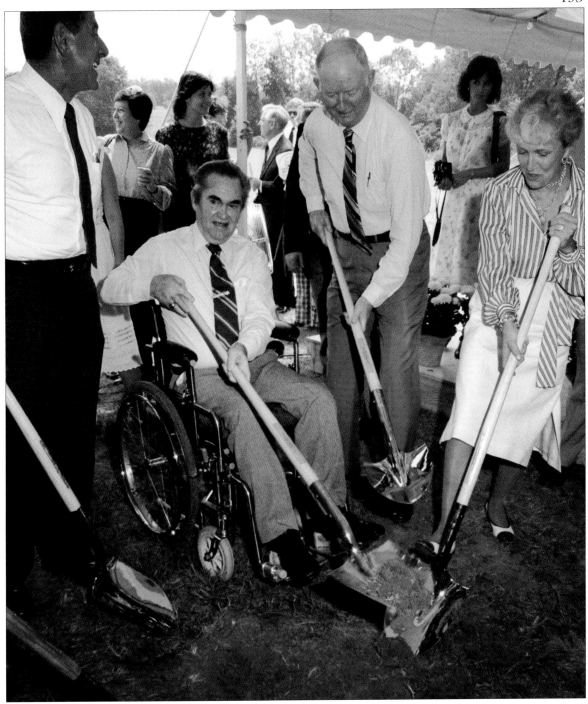

Groundbreaking for the Carolyn Blount Theatre was a joyous occasion. Joining Carolyn and me are Montgomery Mayor Emory Folmar, left, and Alabama Governor George Wallace.

My son, Winton, took charge of construction, directing the project to a timely completion. The Carolyn Blount Theatre had its grand opening years later on December 7, 1985. We kicked off with Shakespeare's *A Midsummer Night's Dream* in the Festival Stage and Tennessee Williams's *The Glass Menagerie* in the Octagon. Actor Tony Randall was the co-master of ceremonies along with our good friend Olivia deHavilland, the great actress. Tony is a very engaging and witty fellow who has an unbelievable passion for the theater. At the opening, he said, "I've seen all of the Shakespeare theaters. None compares to this one." And Dennis Flower, who was chairman of the Royal Shakespeare Theatre, told the gathering, "I'm going to be very cautious, because Englishmen always are. But this is the finest theatrical complex and grounds anytime, anywhere, anyplace."

The Carolyn Blount Theatre is an impossible dream come true. If you had asked any of the management consultants in the arts, they would have told you the idea of building a repertory theater in Alabama was crazy — we didn't have the population base, we didn't have the wealth in this state, it just wouldn't work. But it has worked. The people of Alabama have been incredibly supportive. More than two million people have attended ASF performances since the theater was completed in 1985.

With its modern facilities, built for its particular needs, ASF has grown into quite an operation. It is now the fifth-largest Shakespeare festival in the world and the only year-round professional classical repertory company in the southeastern United States.

Actor Tony Randall, at the podium on the theater steps, was co-host of the dedication ceremonies. Far left is Jane Weinberger, wife of Caspar Weinberger, with whom I had served in the Nixon cabinet. Six people to Tony's left, wearing glasses and leaning forward, is Dennis Flower, chairman of Britain's Royal Shakespeare Theatre. At the ceremonies, Dennis said, "I'm going to be very cautious, because Englishmen always are. But this is the finest theatrical complex and grounds anytime, anywhere, anyplace."

Olivia deHavilland, left, came from Paris to
co-host the dedication ceremonies with
Tony Randall, right. I first met Olivia
through my cousin, Wilda Williams, and we
have been friends for many years. She is a
very bright and talented lady. Here,
Carolyn and I join with Olivia and Tony at
a luncheon the day after the opening.
Even the Queen Mother sent her
congratulations.

CLARENCE HOUSE
S.W.1

I am delighted to learn of the theatre
which has been established in Alabama through
the generosity of Mr. and Mrs. Winton M. Blount,
to be the home of the Alabama Shakespeare
Festival Theatre Company.

This exciting and imaginative initiative
will, I am sure, be welcomed by theatre-lovers
in this country and throughout America, and I
offer my very sincere good wishes for the success
of the venture.

ELIZABETH R
Queen Mother

December 1985

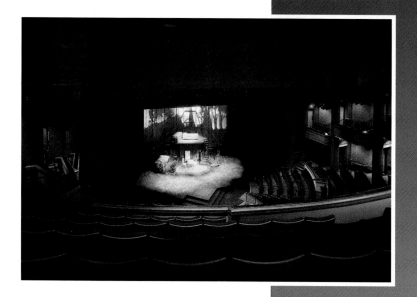

The Carolyn Blount Theatre has been described as "the most beautiful theater building on five continents." Dennis Flower of the Royal Shakespeare Theatre loved our theater so much he presented us with a Royal Shakespeare Theatre flag and asked that we fly it atop our building. We are the only theater in the world, apart from the Royal Shakespeare Theatre itself, authorized to do so. The two photographs, above, show the inside of the 750-seat Festival Stage with the set for *Death of a Salesman*, by Arthur Miller, one of our early productions.

One of the aspects that excites me most is our Children's Theatre and SchoolFest programs, the former for students in grades kindergarten through six, the latter for grades seven through twelve.

It's amazing to watch an audience of young theatergoers. They laugh, they frown, they get involved. We work very hard to turn their experience into one that is both educational and fun. We supply each teacher with study materials and a suggested test related to the play, and after the final curtain comes down the actors return to the stage to rap with the kids. More than 50,000 youngsters a year, from Alabama, Georgia and Florida, attend these lively matinee performances. For a great many, their visit to ASF represents the first time they have ever seen a play. Many of them write to thank us and express their enthusiasm, and we even get letters from parents who are astonished and delighted that their children have been turned on to Shakespeare. And, of course, even as we make a contribution to education in the Southeast, we are building a future audience for ourselves.

The plaque above reads: "This Theatre has been a work of love for Carolyn and me. I have been inspired by her interest and knowledge of Shakespeare and this has guided me in my developing appreciation. It is a privilege for both of us to give this Theatre to the people of the United States and to the generations of the future.
It will stand as an enduring tribute of love to my wife, Carolyn, and it is my desire that it be known forever as The Carolyn Blount Theatre.
  Winton M. Blount
  Dedicated December, 1985"

ASF performs works by many playwrights in addition to Shakespeare. You may be surprised to learn that the single most popular play among the thousands of high school students who have attended our performances is Arthur Miller's tragedy, *Death of a Salesman*, proving just how powerful good theater can be.

One of our most successful — and controversial — productions was *Grover*, which recounted the life of Grover Hall, a 1920s Pulitzer Prize-winning editor from Alabama who battled the KKK as well as his own inner demons. It was written by Randy Hall, Grover's grand nephew. One critic called the work "scary and heartbreaking." However, it was not universally acclaimed, and some people felt we should stick to less controversial fare. Kent Thompson, ASF's artistic director and CEO, countered that part of our mission is to present works that reflect what is going on in society. I agree. ASF's repertoire covers the gamut from light comedy to serious social drama, and hopefully everybody will find something they enjoy. But everybody won't like everything. That's just the nature of theater.

THE WYNTON M. BLOUNT CULTURAL PARK

My original idea, going back to my first meeting with ASF, was to build the theater in Carolyn's and my name. On second thought, I decided to name the theater for Carolyn because she has brought so much joy into my life. The Carolyn Blount Theatre stands as an enduring symbol of my deep love for her.

Carolyn says I am very sentimental, and I guess I am. I am also very good at keeping a secret. I didn't tell her of my decision until two months before the theater opened. When I finally let the cat out of the bag, she was stunned and tried to get me to change my mind. "If you really want to name the theater," she said, "call it the Wynton and Carolyn Blount Theatre." But I was adamant.

About a year after the theater opened, Carolyn had a chance to turn the tables: we decided to develop the grounds around the theater into a cultural park, and she insisted I name the park for myself. Thus was born the Wynton M. Blount Cultural Park. If you're building a shopping center with Macy's at one end, you want J.C. Penney at the other end to attract larger crowds. That was the theory behind the cultural park: we would draw larger audiences by bringing together various cultural activities at one location. The park is the home of the Carolyn Blount Theatre as well as of the Montgomery Museum of Fine Arts, and it is also the site of outdoor concerts on the lawn each summer. We plan to add other facilities, perhaps including an amphitheater.

Carolyn and I found these bronze sheep at a gallery in Colorado and thought they would make a handsome addition to the Alabama Shakespeare Festival's grounds. They are so realistic-looking that many people mistake them for live animals. John Lesenger, the superintendent of our estate, Wynfield, has even gotten phone calls in the middle of the night from people telling him sheep have escaped from our grounds and are grazing on the lawn of ASF.

The park encompasses our original 250-acre site, landscaped with magnolias and poplars on rolling slopes, plus 45 acres I bought in 1995. We own another 60 acres around our home. After we are gone, those 60 acres will become part of the park, and a nonprofit foundation will administer the house and lawns as a museum.

The decision of the Montgomery Museum of Fine Arts to relocate to the park is an interesting story in its own right. Once we embarked on the idea of a cultural park, we thought immediately of attracting the museum. At that time, the museum was housed in a small, inadequate facility in downtown Montgomery, and it had hired a consultant to raise funds for a new building. When the consultant asked me to make a major contribution, I said, "We've got this cultural park. And if the museum will move here, I'll give it 41 of the major paintings from our corporate collection. On top of that, I'll donate half a million dollars." I also said that, while I felt my offer was very attractive, it was up to the museum to decide whether to accept it. I wasn't going to lobby one way or another. I simply was making an offer.

Some of the museum trustees opposed my offer. One of them, Bobby Weil, a very successful cotton broker who had been my finance chairman when I ran for the Senate in 1972, led a group that was partial toward another plan: to build on a piece of land that a wonderful neighbor of mine, Ida Belle Young, was willing to donate. Everybody had the museum's best interests in mind, but as often happens in these cases there were divergent views — some board members favoring the site offered by Ida Belle, others

favoring the nonprofit cultural park. I kept out of the way and didn't say a word. The museum trustees ultimately voted to accept Ida Belle's offer.

A year later, the museum consultant visited me again and said, "There's no way this fund-raising campaign is going to work unless you are involved. Is your offer still open?" I said it was. The trustees then reversed their earlier vote, returned the land to Ida Belle and elected to build in the cultural park. There were a lot of hard feelings about that change of direction, and unfortunately it strained my relations with Bobby Weil. However, Ida Belle was very gracious, as always, and she later donated $800,000 to build a wing at the museum in the cultural park.

The museum's new building, which opened in 1988, sits across the lake from the Carolyn Blount Theatre and is designed in a matching architectural style. Tom Blount served as a consultant to the museum's architects to ensure that the two buildings would complement each other and be compatible with the surrounding grounds. Without a doubt, the Montgomery Museum of Fine Arts is one of the most handsome museum buildings of its size in the world. The museum now attracts more than 120,000 visitors a year, and opposition to its move to the cultural park has just melted away. Many of those who were once critical of this move are now among the biggest supporters

With our modern theater and museum, and with more facilities in the planning stages, I think Montgomery is a model for what a community can accomplish if people get involved.

On a trip to Santa Fe, Carolyn and I met Glenna Goodacre and bought this bronze cast of her delightful work, *The Puddle Jumpers.* We made a gift of the sculpture to the Alabama Shakespeare Festival. It now stands on the theater grounds and is a favorite attraction of visitors. Glenna later won national acclaim for her design of the Women's Vietnam War Memorial in Washington, D.C.

CHAPTER ELEVEN

Everything a Man Could Want

WHEN LAST WE LEFT BLOUNT INTERNATIONAL, Inc., in Chapter Eight, the company had completed the King Saud University project in 1984, acquired Omark Industries in 1985 and sold Washington Steel in 1988. Looking to Blount's future, our goal was to expand in manufacturing, with Omark as our nucleus. However, as discussed in Chapter Eight, we were forced to put our acquisition program temporarily on hold: because we were struggling in the domestic construction business, our balance sheet had weakened and we did not immediately have the resources to purchase additional manufacturing companies.

The late 1980s turned out to be Blount's worst period ever, spiked by a $55 million write-off from continuing operations in fiscal 1989. Never before had we experienced such poor results, nor have we since. And hopefully we never will again. But even as our construction business floundered, dragging down Blount's overall performance, our manufacturing business kept humming right along, generating substantial profits and surpassing construction in revenues in fiscal 1991 for the first time. Manufacturing was our future; construction was not.

In those difficult years when Blount was struggling, I was determined to take whatever steps were necessary to get the company back on a winning track. No company can afford to stand still in today's fast-paced business environment. If you look at successful companies in the 1990s, one trait that consistently stands out is the ability to

Opposite, Carolyn and I pose by the stairway in our home. Left, this painting by John Asaro is one of our favorites in our personal collection. It hangs over the fireplace in our library.

adapt to change. Of course, it is not always clear just when to change or exactly how to do so; making those tough choices lies at the heart of business management.

In fact, we changed successfully, and today Blount's sales and earnings are again rising at a nice clip, surging recently to all-time highs, with fiscal 1996 earnings of $53 million-plus after tax.

Let me tell you how all of this happened — and where Blount is heading as a manufacturing company, one that continues to evolve and to seize on opportunities in its three core markets: outdoor products, industrial and power equipment, and sporting equipment. And, most importantly, one that seeks to create new core businesses on which to build; this is where I will be devoting most of my time in the future.

END OF THE LINE IN CONSTRUCTION

No single change has affected Blount more in the decade of the 1990s than our decision to get out of the construction business. Looking back today, there is no doubt it was the right move for Blount. At the time, however, the decision was filled with anguish and soul-searching. Construction was Blount's heritage. From our beginning in 1946 until the mid-1980s, it was the mainstay of our constantly growing organization. During those 40 years, we built some of the most exciting projects in the world. All of us in the company were extremely proud of our accomplishments.

Why, then, did our construction business fall on hard times? Our problems began in the mid-1980s, when the construction market went into a prolonged downturn. Virtually all the leading contractors in the United States were struggling to earn a decent profit, and any number of contractors went bankrupt.

However, Blount's difficulties went beyond the impact of a poor market. I must acknowledge my own failings. In the early '80s, we were earning so much money on projects in the Middle East that we lost sight of opportunities in the United States. Later in the decade, as the Middle East market softened, we turned our attention back to the United States and sought to recapture volume by bidding aggressively on fixed-price contracts. Attempting to play catch-up in a weak domestic market was disastrous. We got the contracts, all right. But our bids were so low they left little room for surprises or errors, or for profits, resulting in a string of losses.

We were also in the waste-to-energy business, a derivative of construction which we entered in the early 1980s. It was a brand-new industry with great promise, but market demand changed and the tax laws changed, making it less appealing. We sold these operations in 1990-91. We realized that someday waste-to-energy was going to be a good business, but nobody was making any money in it at that time.

Meanwhile, surprisingly, our Middle East construction operations kept going great guns. We were hired for a number of sizable jobs in Kuwait to help rebuild that nation's infrastructure following Operation Desert Storm in 1991. While domestic construction was in terrible shape, international construction, particularly in Kuwait, was very profitable, helping to mitigate our domestic losses.

Bill Van Sant, Blount's president from 1987 to 1991, comes from a manufacturing background and never had much liking for construction. As early as 1989, he recommended we get out as quickly as possible. Considering our protracted losses, perhaps he was right. However, I was not ready to throw in the towel so easily. I loved the construction business. It's high risk. It's exciting. It drove Blount's growth for many years. Deep down inside, I felt we could turn our operations around and recapture the success we had enjoyed in the past. Moreover, we were then building nearly 50 facilities across the United States and in each case were contractually obligated to

Our construction business in the Middle East rebounded when we were hired to rebuild facilities in Kuwait following Operation Desert Storm. Burning in the background is an oil-field fire, set by Iraqi soldiers as they withdrew.

complete the project. Even if we had sold our construction business to someone else and let them finish the jobs, we would have left ourselves open to potentially huge liabilities if the work was not completed satisfactorily.

Seeking to improve our performance, we brought in new management to head our construction division, going through three different executive teams in a period of several years. In addition, we reduced costs relentlessly. And we became more disciplined in our bidding practices. Unfortunately, none of this worked. By 1992, we were still losing money at an alarming rate. At that point, to stem our losses, we stopped bidding on fixed-price projects. This bidding moratorium represented a conscious decision to phase out of construction, even though we did not announce it as such at the time. It would have been foolish and premature to say we were getting out; such an announcement would have crippled our relationships with customers and suppliers and would have made it difficult to rebuild our business if the market outlook suddenly improved.

Because we stopped bidding, by the end of 1993 we were down to half a dozen jobs, all of which were in their final stages. The time had arrived when we could sell our construction business.

Even though I knew we had to sell, and had in fact prepared for this day by scaling back our market presence, it was very difficult emotionally. As I looked back on all those wonderful years in construction, beginning with the purchase of four military surplus Caterpillar tractors in 1946, it was traumatic to think we would no longer be in the business. It may sound like something from a soap

Blount International is today headquartered in this building on Executive Park Drive in Montgomery.

opera — the company founder wanting to hang onto a business he loves so much. But I think anybody who has built a company can understand exactly how I felt.

In late 1993, as we got ready to exit construction, I had a cardiovascular problem. Almost certainly it was related to the stress of the sale. I went to the University of Alabama medical center in Birmingham for an angioplasty. Shortly after the procedure was completed, and while I was still in the hospital, I had another attack. Ed Varner, my stepson, who is a very successful gynecologist, was in the room and immediately told the nurses to put me on oxygen. One nurse said, "Doctor, are you taking responsibility for this?" He said, "Yes, I take full responsibility." It's hard to tell for sure, but his intervention may have saved my life. I was fortunate to receive the very best medical care and have now recovered fully.

I got through that medical crisis and sold the business without further incident. From the start, the logical buyer was John Caddell, about whom I have talked earlier in this book. John was a 31-year Blount employee who rose to the presidency of our construction division. He is like a feisty bulldog: hard-working, relentless, never misses a beat. I had fired John in 1983 for reasons I later regretted. We gave him a substantial termination agreement, which helped him start his own company, Caddell Construction. He has been very successful. Even though John and I parted company on traumatic terms, he did not hold any grudges. His last words to me, after getting over the emotional impact of being fired, were, "Well, I hope you haven't made a mistake." My first words to him when we got back together years later were, "I did make a mistake."

We might have tried to sell our construction operations at auction. But there was not a big market for construction companies, given the state of the industry. I said, "It would be a whole lot better to sell to John. He knows our business, and he knows our people and will take care of them."

John and I got down to serious negotiations in the fall of 1993. We met initially in Bangkok, where we were both attending an industry conference, and then spent four days at my home in Montgomery hammering out a deal. After we shook hands, we drove over to Blount's headquarters to announce the agreement to the employees in our construction division. John and I had worked closely together for years building Blount's construction business. Moreover, when John was president of the division, he had hired many of the people who were in that room when we made our announcement. He still felt very connected to Blount and its construction operations. As he said later, "I told somebody the other day how much Blount meant to me, and he said, 'But Red fired you.' And I said, 'You don't wipe out a 30-year relationship in one day.'" It was an emotional moment for both of us—announcing that Blount had reached the end of the line in construction.

Today, with the perspective of time, I feel very good about the sale. It was obviously the right thing to do, for our company, our shareholders and our employees. And once I got over the initial anguish, I felt like a burden had been lifted from my shoulders.

In my office and my home, I still display many mementos of Blount's years in construction. I am very proud of what we accomplished. It is something that will always be part of me.

BLOUNT TODAY: GROWTH IN MANUFACTURING

Our decision to concentrate on manufacturing is paying off handsomely. Blount has entered a new phase of growth, as demonstrated by a dramatic upswing in financial results to new highs in fiscal 1996.

Morover, our recent financial performance has been good news for Blount shareholders, who have seen the market value of their stock soar more than 500 percent during the past three years in response to our rising earnings.

In the case of B. F. Shaw, J. P. Burroughs, Washington Steel, Omark and many smaller operations, we demonstrated our ability to acquire a company and add value by improving its returns and quality. With Omark as our base, we have been acquiring other companies, starting with Dixon Industries in 1990. Headquartered in Coffeyville, Kansas, Dixon makes zero-turning-radius riding lawnmowers. It was founded in 1973 by an inventor named K. O. Dixon who sold it to the Coleman Company, famous for its Coleman lamps. Coleman was, in turn, swallowed up by financier Ronald Perelman. However, Perelman did not want Dixon and tried to sell it for nearly a year. We finally came along and bought it for the advantageous price of $25 million. Within three years, we received an offer of $50 million, but turned it down. Dixon is a small company compared to the John Deeres and Toros of the world, but it is very profitable and growing, recording its 16th consecutive year of increased sales in fiscal 1996.

Dixon Industries manufactures zero-turning-radius riding lawnmowers, recognized as the standard of excellence in the lawn care market. Founder K. O. Dixon stayed at the helm after we acquired the company in 1990 and has guided it to continued strong growth.

K.O. Dixon still runs it for us, although he is retiring this year and we have named a successor, John Mowder, a longtime employee.

Our game plan is to continue to acquire companies where we can add value by applying our skills in manufacturing technology, distribution know-how, product development and customer service. Since purchasing Dixon, we have made four additional acquisitions.

In March 1991, we acquired Gear Products, Inc., Tulsa, Oklahoma, which makes rotation bearings and mechanical power transmission components. These products are used in our forestry and industrial equipment operations and are sold also to other original equipment manufacturers.

In April 1994, we bought CTR Manufacturing, Union Grove, North Carolina, which makes timber processing equipment. CTR expands the total timber harvesting and handling system that Blount offers to the forestry industry.

In November 1994, we acquired Ram-Line, Inc., Grand Junction, Colorado, which manufactures stocks, magazines, lens caps and other products for the shooting sports market.

And in December 1995, we completed the acquisition of Simmons Outdoor Corporation, Tallahassee, Florida, which makes rifle scopes, binoculars, telescopes and other outdoor sports items. According to *Gun World* magazine, Simmons is one of the fastest-growing companies in the shooting products field.

The combined price for these four businesses — Gear Products, CTR, Ram-Line and Simmons — was $73 million. Going forward, we have substantial cash reserves to buy additional companies in niche

The "new" Blount manufactures exciting, best-in-the-world products with leading market shares. Our core businesses are outdoor products, industrial and power equipment, and sporting equipment. We market our products in 130 countries.

markets that fit with our core operations. We remain open, as well, to the idea of a large acquisition if the right deal were to come along. At the same time, we will continue to build our existing operations through product development, market expansion and international growth. Our plan calls for 15 percent of each year's total sales to come from new products introduced in the prior three years.

We not only have great products and significant cash reserves, but we also have a strong group of experienced operating managers to put our strategies into action.

Our Oregon Cutting Systems Division (OCSD) is led by Jim Osterman, a 37-year employee of Omark and Blount. Jim spent 12 years as head of the European operations of Omark and, since his appointment to the presidency of OCSD in 1987, has led the division to its current status as a world-class manufacturing organization with nearly $250 million in sales.

Darrel Inman is president of our Sporting Equipment Division. Prior to assuming that position in 1995, he was the division's vice president-engineering and, before that, vice president and general manager of its Lewiston operations.

Don Zorn, president of our Forestry & Industrial Equipment Division, joined Blount in 1994. He previously was president and chief operating officer of Grove Cranes, a division of Grove Worldwide Company in Shady Grove, Pennsylvania. He has done a tremendous job of leading this division to record sales and profits.

I am very pleased with Blount's prospects in manufacturing.

Saw chain and saw bar are the two principal products of our Oregon Cutting Systems Division. Sales continue to increase not only in the United States but also overseas. International markets now account for more than 60 percent of the division's revenues.

JOHN PANETTIERE'S LEADERSHIP OF BLOUNT

Blount is led today by John Panettiere, our president and chief executive officer. I continue as board chairman, but am no longer as active in day-to-day business decisions.

I have always believed that hiring good people is the key to business success. We found John in 1992 through an executive search firm. As John recounts, he was sitting at home on a Wednesday night in Williamsport, Maryland, when he received an unexpected call from a representative of the search consultant. Although John wasn't looking to change jobs, he agreed to come to Montgomery to have lunch with me. We sent our company plane for him and had it stand by to fly him back to Maryland after we finished our meal. However, John and I got so wrapped up in our conversation that we kept talking until after 5 p.m. About a month later, John returned to Montgomery with his wife, Wendy, for a three-day weekend to learn more about Blount and talk with our senior executives. It was a whirlwind courtship. We had interviewed several candidates prior to John, but decided very quickly he was our choice based on his proven record in manufacturing. John says he did not come to Montgomery on that second trip prepared to take the job. But I offered it to him, and he accepted on Sunday before he left.

John and his wife are both originally from Kansas City. Before joining Blount as president and chief operating officer, he spent his career at automobile companies such as Ford, American Motors and Fiat-Allis, and then with Grove Worldwide Company, which manufactures hydraulic cranes. He was extremely successful as CEO of Grove, running a $600-million-a-year business and improving its profits dramatically. Grove was owned by Hanson PLC, a huge British company.

John is an entirely different type of senior executive than we have ever before had at Blount. He is more in the mold of what I call the modern-day manufacturing manager, such as Jack Welch of General Electric — hard-nosed, cost-conscious, bottom-line oriented. You see a lot of these executives around the country today because of the intense competitive pressures of a global economy.

There was some clash between John's numbers-oriented culture and my people-oriented culture the first year he was with Blount. But we talked about that, sometimes in a rather spirited manner, and worked out our differences, arriving at a management style

John Panettiere joined us in 1992 as president and chief operating officer and was elected chief executive officer the following year. John's outstanding background with such companies as Grove Worldwide, Fiat-Allis, American Motors, Chrysler and Ford makes him ideally suited to lead Blount as a manufacturing company. He is doing a terrific job.

that I think incorporates the best of both. In June 1993, in recognition of his significant accomplishments, John was elected CEO.

John and Wendy have settled into Montgomery as if they had lived here all their lives. John is a great family man, and he loves the outdoors. He is doing a wonderful job for Blount. We are fortunate to have him. He is the right person at the right time, leading Blount in its new direction of expansion in manufacturing. He has the fire and capacity to continue to aggressively seek acquisitions. With John as CEO, the company is in very capable hands.

EVERYTHING A MAN COULD WANT

Blount's shares became listed on the New York Stock Exchange on November 6, 1995. Our NYSE listing gives us greater corporate visibility and provides increased liquidity for our shareholders.

This book began with my youth and has continued through the 50th anniversary of Blount International, Inc. I did not found Blount with any elaborate management theories. I was just a young man who was determined to work hard and take chances. I think, also, that I had the integrity to make people feel comfortable doing business with me because they felt I would always keep my word. And I was fortunate to grow up in a family that believed very much in the American dream — the idea that anybody can accomplish anything if they set their mind to it.

I am sometimes asked whether it would be possible to build another Blount International starting from scratch. My answer, of course, is, "Absolutely." I say to young people: If I could do it, maybe you could, too. I have never seen so much opportunity as there is today — the growth of global markets, the advance of technology, the rise of free enterprise around the world and the fundamental optimism of Americans about the future of our great nation. These are truly exciting times.

Moreover, across the land, there is growing public recognition that America's prosperity does not come from government or from untapped natural resources, but from the ingenuity of people working together to build successful businesses. Blount is a vivid example. Its history shows how a company can take root and prosper in a free society — providing useful products and services, creating jobs, paying taxes, supporting the growth of suppliers and contributing to the economic well-being of the community. Blount's success reflects the efforts of many, many people — from our very first employees, James Griffin, Frazier Pair and Sam Wilson, to the thousands of others who have followed, each making a vital contribution. When you come right down to it, this book is about Blount people and the company they have created by working together toward a common purpose. I wish I could name every one of our employees in this book. That is not possible. But I do want to thank each of you for a job well done.

My life has been fun and fulfilling beyond my wildest expectations. And it still is. I continue not only as chairman of Blount International, but remain active also in a number of nonprofit organizations, such as Success by Six, the Alabama Shakespeare Festival, the Folger Shakespeare Library, the American Enterprise Institute, Rhodes College and the National Actors Theatre, among others. However, I am working a bit less than I used to, taking more time to smell the roses. Carolyn and I enjoy traveling, getting together with friends and visiting our children and grandchildren.

But I never want to quit working altogether. "Retirement" is not in my vocabulary. I always want to be active in something, whether it be business or community service. I enjoy being involved far too much ever to stop.

Wait a minute — a new acquisition has just popped up and I had better see what we can do about it. This is fun.

— 30 —

Blount International, Inc., Board of Directors

Directors (from left to right) are: Alfred M. Gleason, John M. Panettiere, Joab L. Thomas, Oscar J. Reak (retired from board in 1994), H. Corbin Day, Herbert J. Dickson, W. Houston Blount, Winton M. Blount, C. Todd Conover, Mary D. Nelson and James W. Hargrove (advisory director). Not pictured are Gene Cartledge, Emory Folmar, Art Ronan, Admiral Thomas Moorer (advisory director).

OUR COMPANY has been blessed with having had many superb individuals on its board of directors. From the beginning, the Blount board has been a very involved group, taking a hands-on role.

Blount grew rapidly from the start, and in 1964 I asked Dillard Munford to become our first outside director. I had met Dillard through the Young Presidents Organization (YPO), and we became great friends. Dillard owned Munford, Inc., in Atlanta and had been president of YPO. He was a great character, a great story-teller and had terrific insights about people. Dillard served as a director and advisory director of Blount for 29 years, dying in 1993 after a brief illness. I miss him very much.

In 1966, Herb Dickson joined our board and continues as a member today, with the longest service apart from my brother,

Houston, and me. In selecting directors, we have always sought individuals with particular expertise of value to Blount. Herb was a senior executive of Citizens & Southern Bank in Atlanta, handling our business, and was very familiar with our corporate objectives and financial needs.

Blount went public in 1972 while I was on leave in government service. As a public company, we expanded our board to include more outside directors. Two of the first additions were highly talented individuals who had been members of my post office management team — David Nelson and Jim Hargrove.

David is an attorney who was the principal person in charge of drafting the Postal Reform Act.

When David was appointed a federal judge by President Reagan, resigning his board seat, I asked his wife, Mary Nelson, to become a director of our company. Mary is president of Nelson & Co., consulting actuaries, in Cincinnati. She has been on our board since 1986 and continues to play an active role.

Jim Hargrove had been my assistant postmaster general for finance and administration. Prior to joining the Post Office Department, he had been senior vice president of Eastern Gas Transmission, and after his post office service, he was President Ford's Ambassador to Australia. He retired recently from our board after 21 years. He continues as an advisory director.

Admiral Tom Moorer, who was chairman of the U.S. Joint Chiefs of Staff from 1970 through 1974, was elected to our board in 1974. He was a great addition and was someone I often turned to for advice. He and his wife, Carrie, were both from Eufaula, Alabama, and Tom had risen through the Navy to assume leadership of the largest and most powerful armed forces in the world. He retired from our board in 1992 and, like Jim, continues as an advisory director.

Joab Thomas is one of the nation's leading educators. We worked closely together when I was a trustee of the University of Alabama and he was president of the University of Alabama, Tuscaloosa. He became a director of Blount in 1981. I was sorry to lose him at the university when he became president of Penn State University in 1990, but I was delighted that he stayed on the board of Blount.

Al Gleason and Bob Adams joined our board in 1985, when we acquired Omark Industries. Both had been Omark directors. Al was later CEO of PacifiCorp, a major electric utility company in the Northwest, and is now Commission President at the Port of Portland in Portland, Oregon. He asked that he not stand for reelection in June of 1996 as he was heavily involved in Oregon. Bob was the number three executive at 3M Company. He died prematurely only a few years after becoming a director of Blount. It was a terrible loss.

Corbin Day became a director of Blount in 1992. He had been a senior partner of Goldman Sachs and is chairman of Jemison Investment Co. in Birmingham. As is true of many of our directors, he serves on a number of boards in addition to that of Blount, bringing extensive personal experience to the corporate governance process.

Todd Conover also joined our board in 1992. Todd is president and CEO of the Vantage Company and serves on the board of PacifiCorp. He was recommended to me by Al Gleason.

Another 1992 addition was John Panettiere, who was elected to the board when he became Blount's president and chief operating officer. He was elected CEO the following year. As I have said many times in this book, John is doing a wonderful job leading Blount in its dramatic growth in manufacturing.

Art Ronan is a long-time friend of John Panettiere. A former president, automotive operations, at Rockwell International Corp., he joined our board in 1993.

In 1994, I asked Gene Cartledge, who had been CEO of Union Camp Corporation, to become a member of the Blount board of directors. I had served on the Union Camp board for 20 years and knew first-hand of Gene's extraordinary abilities.

Emory Folmar is the most recent addition to our board of directors, having been elected in 1995. Emory has been mayor of Montgomery since 1977, doing a wonderful job. His election to our board brings an important new perspective to our deliberations — that of our relationship to the community.

Acknowledgments

THE IDEA FOR THIS BOOK originated with my wife, Carolyn. For years, she encouraged me to put the story of my business and my life on paper. I have finally done it, with her love and support.

I also had the support of my collaborator and friend, Dick Blodgett, whose professionalism, insight and attention to detail made this project both easier and more enjoyable than it otherwise could have been.

Many people made invaluable contributions by sharing their recollections and insights. I would especially like to thank my children and stepchildren: Winton, Tom, Sam and Joe Blount, Kay Blount Miles, Ed Varner and his wife, Pam Varner and Stuart Varner King. My cousin, Wilda Williams, helped recall events from our childhood in Union Springs.

Governor George Wallace was kind enough to spend time discussing Alabama politics. Dr. Phil Austin, chancellor of the University of Alabama, shared some of his thoughts about the changes that have taken place at the university. Many of Blount International's current and former executives, including John Caddell, Frank McFadden, Joe McInnes, John Panettiere, Sam Wilson and W. E. "Bull" Wilson, provided their perspective on events in the company's history, as did Tom Carruthers of our law firm, Bradley Arant, and Bob Bleke of Bleke & Boyd. Admiral Tom Moorer, for many years a member of Blount's board of directors, also gave generously of his time and ideas.

In researching the chapter on postal reform, I was helped by Paul Carlin and Noel Koch, who were key members of my Post Office Department management team.

Others who have provided invaluable assistance include Mary Katherine Blount, Bill Chandler, Peter Flanigan, Larry Fleischman, Don Kendall, John Lesenger and Kent Thompson, each of whom is identified in this book.

I especially wish to thank my executive assistant, Shirley Milligan, who helped guide this book to fruition. She was a tower of strength through many months of work.

WINTON M. "RED" BLOUNT
April 1996

Index

Bold listings indicate illustrated material.